LEADING

Your Business

FORWARD

LEADING
Your Business
FORWARD

=== ALIGNING ===
GOALS, PEOPLE, AND SYSTEMS
FOR SUSTAINABLE SUCCESS

SHANE A. YOUNT
JOHN M. PYECHA
WITH
ANNA VERSTEEG
SETH DAVIES
LINDA SEGALL

New York   Chicago   San Francisco   Lisbon   London
Madrid   Mexico City   Milan   New Delhi   San Juan
Seoul   Singapore   Sydney   Toronto

1 2 3 4 5 6 7 8 9 10   QFR/QFR   1 9 8 7 6 5 4 3

ISBN   978-0-07-181713-4
MHID   0-07-181713-1

e-ISBN   978-0-07-181714-1
e-MHID   0-07-181714-X

McGraw-Hill books are available at special quantity discounts to use as premiums and sales promotions or for use in corporate training programs. To contact a representative, please e-mail us at bulksales@mcgraw-hill.com.

This book is printed on acid-free paper.

Contents

Contents

Acknowledgments

Shane, John, Anna, and Seth would like to take this opportunity to sincerely thank those individuals who have allowed us to enjoy our overwhelming success—our clients. Over the last 22 years we have had the pleasure of working with some of the best leaders and organizations in the world. The opportunity to play a small part in helping the world's most-recognized companies achieve performance excellence is both humbling and rewarding. Every engagement has presented us with opportunities to grow both personally and professionally, and for that we are grateful. It is no secret that for a consulting company to thrive for 22 years it must have a methodology that is both compelling and impactful, because, at the end of the day, that methodology must deliver sustainable value. So to our clients, we thank you for your trust, your commitment, and most of all your friendship.

Lastly, no enterprise succeeds without the support and dedication of those people who are behind the scenes. We would like to thank our spouses—Stephanie Yount, Lynn Pyecha, Ron VerSteeg, and Ann Davies. Without their encouragement, support, and abundant patience, our

22-year run would not have been nearly so successful nor enjoyable.

We hope you enjoy this book and find that the contents contained within allow you to plot a successful course utilizing your own leadership GPS!

Introduction

"Gabby," the feminine name we have given to our global positioning system (GPS) manufactured by Garmin Industries, is quite remarkable. In her soft-spoken yet insistent manner, she guides us through the spaghetti bowls of metropolitan intersections, across the deserts of the Southwest, and through the mazes of streets in both large and small metropolises. She isn't infallible, yet she invariably gets us to where we want to go.

Of course, for her to do what she is supposed to do, we need first to tell her our destination—along with, perhaps, some parameters, such as "shortest route," "scenic route," "no tolls," "no ferries," and "major highways only."

And we need to keep her maps up to date.

If we fail to do any of those things, Gabby will let us down, and we may become temporarily lost. Even if we keep our end of the bargain, sometimes as we are driving along we miss a turn. Gabby insistently tells us she is "recalculating." And she continues to recalculate until we accept her directions and get back on route.

We love Gabby. She has become an invaluable friend and aid to us as we explore new places. She has almost (but not quite) replaced all of our printed maps. We quite literally feel lost without her.

In the business world, over the years, business leaders have been given a number of different roadmaps to success. Total Quality Management (TQM), Lean Manufacturing Systems, ISO, Total Preventive Maintenance (TPM), and Six Sigma, to name a few, all promised us how-to solutions to business growth. They were good maps, yet, with few exceptions, they did not guide us to a sustainable level of success.

What has been missing is a GPS for leaders. With Gabby as an inspiration, we have written *Leading Your Business Forward*, which we consider a Gabby for business.

In this book, we lay out the process of a *leadership* GPS, using Gabby as our guide. The book is organized into five sections, with which (if you use a GPS in your car) you will be familiar:

Section 1: Acquiring

Section 2: Settings

Section 3: Where To?

Section 4: Recalculating

Section 5: Arriving!

Within each of these sections—which act as steps to implementing leadership GPS— you'll set your direction, give your leadership Gabby parameters, and follow her directions. And, using leadership GPS, you'll attain that next level you've always wanted and tried to achieve—sustainable success.

ACQUIRING

Traveling—whether across country or across the city—is much easier today than it was a mere decade ago.

Back then, in the "olden days," if you were going somewhere previously unknown to you, you had to either call ahead to get elaborate directions from someone at your destination or you had to consult a map and hope you could remember every turn, especially if you didn't have a navigator with you in the car. Even if you used *both* methods, the likelihood was high that you would make some wrong turns along the way.

Since the mid- to late 2000s, when global positioning systems (GPSs) became commercially feasible and affordable, taking a trip has become much more efficient. Plug in the portable unit, enter into the GPS where you want to go, and within seconds you are given both verbal and visual directions to your destination. The GPS will even tell you if you are going off course.

What an invention!

Technology, of course, is the basis of how the GPS system works. Before the GPS (we call ours Gabby) can give you directions, it has to *acquire satellites* to locate exactly where you are. The device in your car transmits and receives signals from several of the 24 GPS satellites that precisely orbit the earth twice a day. When your GPS unit communicates with four or more of these satellites, it determines your exact longitude, latitude, and altitude and then plots that information on an electronic map. Once Gabby knows *where* you are, she can calculate other information that could be helpful to you, such as how fast you are driving, how far you have driven, and what time you should arrive at your destination.

Obviously, "acquiring a signal"—the first function Gabby undertakes upon activation—is critical. Without knowing your exact location, she can do nothing else.

Section 1: Acquiring in *Leading Your Business Forward* comprises three chapters, which all share the common theme of "acquiring." In management terms, think of acquiring as pinpointing your leadership status by making an assessment— that is, *determining a baseline* of where you and your organization are so that you can set a direction (goals) and measure results to get to where you want to go—sustained success. The chapters in this section are as follows:

Chapter 1: What's the Status of Your Goals?

Chapter 2: How Engaged Are Your People?

Chapter 3: Do you Have Leadership Systems in Place?

With the information you learn in Section 1 of *Leading Your Business Forward* you will be ready to set your direction for sustainable success.

What's the Status of Your Goals?

Vacations are a time to let go of all worries and stresses. To get away from it all, some people just get in the car, turn on the ignition, and leave their cares behind. They make no plans; they travel where the road takes them. Their vacations are spontaneous and adventuresome.

When these same people take a business trip, however, it's another story. They abandon spontaneity. When they have a meeting set up with an important client, they make sure they get to their appointment on time. They plan the trip down to the last detail, allowing for contingencies. When they get into their car, they plug in their GPS and—after the GPS acquires their current location—set their destination, and take off, confident to arrive at their meeting place on time.

Our work throughout the last 20 years has taken us into the depths of all types of organizations. We have learned through observation, surveys, and other studies that organizations meriting the descriptor "high-performing" share three essential components. Not coincidentally the three components shared by all high-performing organizations—goals, people, and systems—are the three "satellites" in *Leading Your Business Forward: Aligning Goals, People, and Systems for Sustainable Success.*

Goals—the first of three GPS "satellites"—sets the direction as well as the destination for high performance. Let's look at how these successful organizations differentiate themselves from all others through their goal-setting processes.

Everyone "knows" that goals having a clearly defined vision, mission, and strategic direction are essential to business operations. What is often missing, however, is how to link tactical operational goals to the strategic direction. Goal setting has been a staple of business operations for decades. Unfortunately, however, goal setting in itself is not a panacea to an ailing organization. Goals are great, but unless goals are established with a *business focus*, and *everyone* has a clear understanding of them, accepts *accountability* for achieving them, and pursues them with a sense of *urgency*, goals are just sentences written on a piece of paper. Consider this example:

A well-kept secret

A number of years ago, the vice president of human resources at a diversified, midsized manufacturing company saw a problem: Top management at both the corporate and the division levels was "graying," but the company had no plan in place to groom individuals to take over leadership positions in the organization. What would happen if the company experienced an exodus of executives to retirement, which could potentially happen within just a few years?

The VP decided something had to be done, and he presented the idea of developing a succession plan to the company's president. After receiving an OK, the HR department undertook the succession-planning task by identifying success factors for each of the key positions, selecting possible candidates to fill slots, and listing the types of experience and training candidates would need to become qualified to take on advanced leadership responsibilities.

The succession-planning project took months of concentrated effort to complete. When the results were compiled in a confidential report, the VP presented it to the president, who said it looked like a fine plan and told the VP of HR his department should update it annually. The VP of HR took the task to heart and developed candidates to succeed him when he retired.

When the VP of HR did retire some years later, his successor (who had been groomed according to plan) found a copy of the succession plan. As she visited with each of the company's top leaders, she included it on her agenda for discussion. She would ask, "According to the succession plan, I see that your goal is to develop [names] as potential candidates to take over for you when you retire. How are they being prepared for future responsibilities?"

She was shocked to hear the same response from each of her internal clients: "We have succession-planning goals? I didn't know that. I didn't know I needed to do anything."

The new HR executive learned that, although the succession plan looked good on paper, it had been developed without the input of those it affected. As a result, no one had committed to it, and the company was essentially at the same place it had been when the concept of succession planning had first been discussed. The succession plan had been a well-kept secret.

We have found that in high-performing organizations, *everyone* in the organization—from the president down to the janitor—has a robust and thorough understanding of whether the organization is winning or losing. They have this understanding, because of the following:

- Goal setting is not an annual exercise taken lightly. It is a serious process shared by everyone in the organization.

- The organization's goals are crystal clear to everyone.

- The organization's goals are business focused, with measureable business results.

- The metrics that depict where the organization stands relative to its goals are easy to use and grasp.

- The organization's systems *allow and encourage* each team member and every team to influence goal attainment.

- Everyone works with a sense of accountability and urgency to meet these goals.

In high-performing organizations, goals are not abstract; they are relevant to the overall organization as well as to the various teams and individuals on those teams. This is because goals are developed systematically, using information that comes from the bottom up as well as the top down. They are always *business focused*.

No Secrets

A consumer-products company in North Carolina does something that could be held up as a best practice: Every Monday morning when team members come to work, they see 32 pieces of paper posted in the foyer of the employee entrance. The top piece of paper gives the status of the company—where it is to date in meeting its goals. The other papers depict each team's contributions to meeting their goals. Everyone knows if the company is winning or losing by virtue of broadcasting its status and the status of each team through the use of a business scorecard built on business-focused goals.

Something else that happens, however, is just as important: If the company is missing a goal, team members can see the scorecards of every other team. They know which team is meeting (or exceeding) goals, and which teams are missing them. The scorecards and their public display create accountability for everyone to work together for mutual success.

7

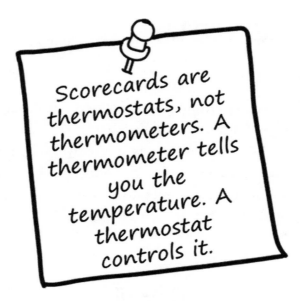

Figure 1-1 Scorecards Are Thermostats

How do high-performing organizations achieve this level of goal setting? Their secret is to track progress toward goal achievement systematically *through business-focused score-cards*. Scorecards are one of the systems our leadership GPS system uses to align goals throughout the organization. *(More on using business-focused scorecards later.)*

Business-focused scorecards are system tools that educate, facilitate, and motivate as follows:

- **Educate.** Because scorecards are developed around a set of key business areas (such as quality, safety, cost, productivity, people, and customer service), they create a common language that everyone in the organization learns and uses. Additionally, because team members participate in building and reporting on their scorecards, they gain a greater understanding of what metrics are, how they are linked to the organization's strategy, and what behaviors and factors affect performance both positively and negatively. The result: Even an associate at the lowest level of the organization can look at the corporate scorecard and understand what it says.

- **Facilitate.** Weekly meetings in high-performing organizations are focused around the business scorecard, with teams discussing what went well during the last week and what did not go so well — and the corrective actions they need to take to get back on course.

- **Motivate.** Teams develop their own goals, objectives, and corrective action plans in support of the corporate goals. They relish their accountability to achieve and take pride in celebrating when goals reach the "green" state.

Business-focused scorecards used in high-performing organizations are not mere thermometers that tell at a glance if an organization is winning or losing. Rather, scorecards in these organizations are thermostats. The difference between a thermometer and a thermostat? A thermometer is static and only tells "what is." In contrast, a thermostat not only tells us the current temperature, it adjusts itself to bring the temperature up or down to the desired level! High-performing organizations use their business-focused scorecards as thermostats—always adjusting for optimal output.

When business-focused scorecards are used as thermostats, people feel connected to their jobs and the organization. The scorecards are the critical link to engagement. And engagement is critical to sustained success.

In the true anecdote, "A well-kept secret," the company could easily have made inroads on achieving its succession-planning goals by including the department managers in the goal-development process. And the written goals should have been specific, measurable, achievable, relevant (business-focused), and timely (SMART) for each department. (*More on this in Chapter 8.*) Most importantly, the goals could have been achieved if everyone in the organization had been accountable to achieve them.

Common sense says you can't get to where you want to go unless you know your starting place. In the business world, you can't know if you are winning or losing without knowing your starting status. So the first "satellite" the leadership GPS process "acquires" is getting a fix on the organization's goals, *as they currently stand*—as measured against those that are known to be high performers.

Assessment: "Acquiring" your fix on business-focused goals

When our car's GPS "fires" up, it identifies our specific longitude, latitude, and altitude coordinates and electronically maps them to locate us. The following assessment will help you "acquire" your fix on your organization's business-focused goals:

Instructions: Check off each statement that is true for you and/or your organization.

1. Your organization's goals are published and available to all team members.

2. The goals are published on a business scorecard that is updated weekly.

3. You can recite your company's/department's primary goals without hesitation.

4. Without looking at a chart, you can report the status of your organization—whether it is winning or losing.

5. Each of your team members can tell you the status of the organization—whether it is winning or losing.

6. When you develop goals, you do it based on desired outcomes as well as observed deficiencies.

7. When you develop goals, you do it with the input of those affected by the goals; you alone do not develop goals for others.

8. You prioritize daily and weekly activities based on business goals.

9. Measuring goal attainment is simple and easy for you.

10. Your goals—the company's, the department's, the team's, and your own—are all written clearly, using SMART criteria.

11. You can ascertain the status of the business (whether it is winning or losing) within five seconds of reviewing your scorecard.

12. You are never surprised when you receive published performance results.

What is your fix on your business-focus goals?

7 or fewer "true" answers—You are off course. Please adjust your settings.

8–10 "true" answers—Detour ahead. Calculate an alternative route.

11–12 "true" answers—You are on course. You will arrive at your destination successfully.

Comment: As you begin implementing your leadership GPS process you will probably find that many of these statements do not currently apply to your organization. Our leadership GPS process will help solve this situation. Revisit this checklist after you have implemented leadership GPS in your organization.

CHAPTER 2

How Engaged Are Your People?

The second "satellite" that leadership GPS "acquires" is people.

A phenomenon we have observed in high-performing organizations is noteworthy: The people in these organizations—*at all levels*—are motivated. They work with urgency, accountability, and a true sense of direction. They *want* to do a good job, and because their goals (as well as the organization's) are clearly spelled out, they *know* if they are doing a good job or if they are missing the mark. (And if they are missing the mark, they take steps to get back on track.) There's no guesswork involved in assessing their performance.

In one word, the team members in these organizations are *engaged*.

An example of an engaged workforce

A privately held company and a large producer of frost-free evaporator coils is also a leading global supplier of aluminum heat-transfer tubing and components for appliances, HVAC, and automotive air conditioning systems.

Not satisfied with the status quo, several years ago the leaders at this company decided the way to improve and sustain their success was by engaging their associates through teamwork and implementing our method of Process-Based Leadership (PBL). Team members became engaged and accountable through *weekly communication meetings* focused on performance, business *scorecards* for every team, team *problem solving* to resolve performance issues and make improvements, and *auditable processes* to drive business results.

During a six-year period following implementation, during which time engagement soared, this company's sales tripled and its profits grew by an astounding 260%!

Having an engaged workforce does pay off. Studies have shown that businesses having a workforce of highly engaged associates outperform their peers by as much as 28%. That's pretty impressive. More sobering is the fact that companies whose employees have a low level of engagement experience a *decline* in operating income of more than 32% (2008 Towers Perrin Global Workplace Study).

What is really scary, however, is that *low engagement begets low performance* because the poor performers actually set performance expectations for the organization! In other words, when a company tolerates poor performance (that is, its workers are unengaged), high performers (highly engaged associates) throw in the towel,

Figure 2-1 Low Engagement Begets

saying, "Why should I work so hard? I don't get anything more than Terry who barely works at all." When expectations go from "I'll give as much as I can to help the company succeed" to "I'll do what I have to to keep my job" it is no wonder companies with low engagement experience declines in income.

A Broken Engagement

Tom, a typical first-line leader in a manufacturing plant, has 15 team members under his supervision. Like so many other supervisors, he has a lot on his plate, but he feels fortunate that he can depend on three of his top performers whenever he gets in a bind. Whenever the department falls behind on its productivity or quality, or if a special project comes down, he asks these three individuals to pitch in.

Tom has noticed, however, that in the last couple of months, these three top performers have seemed reluctant to do "more." They say "yes" to a project, then take their time on getting it done. Tom wonders what is going on. His "stars" aren't shining any more brightly than any of the other team members. They don't volunteer, and their energy level has declined. Worse, yet, now that the economy has picked up and jobs are more plentiful, one of these individuals said she was updating her résumé.

What Does Engagement Look Like?

We define "engagement" as associates who are completely involved in their work. They have an emotional as well as an intellectual attachment to their organization, their coworkers, and the work they perform. Their interest level and desire to do well at work go beyond mere enthusiasm. They can be likened to having a passion to do "right."

Engaged associates take deliberate, demonstrative actions to get the job done on time and with purpose, knowing that what they are doing contributes to the employer's success. And they can tell you if the company is winning or losing. They participate in order to advance the business.

A few years ago, a popular buzzword flitting around the corporate world was "empowerment." To empower employees is to give them the tools and authority to do the job. No doubt about it: Empowerment is desirable and good; but empowerment has to be done right. Unless team members are engaged at the same time they are empowered, little will occur. You will just have unproductive employees who have tools and authority but no commitment to contribute.

At the height of the "empowerment frenzy," many employers hastened to put into place programs that resulted in making employees *feel* good about working for the organization. This type of empowerment is not engagement. Engagement is not about making people happy or creating a great place to work. That's not to say the work environment should be unfriendly and cold. Of course you want team members to brag about where they work! But engagement is more than that. Engagement is about bringing people together with a unity of business purpose and holding them accountable to helping the organization achieve its goals.

What causes people to become engaged (and as a consequence, to use their empowerment)? Our studies in high-performing organizations show that associates become engaged when they

- are consistently held accountable,
- are business-focused, and
- are led by process-based leaders.

When these three things are integrated and occur concurrently, not only do employees become engaged team members and associates, the business succeeds. Feelings are important, but they don't create success. Actions that move the business forward make the organization succeed.

Don't be mistaken: There *is* a correlation between *feeling* and *doing*. When associates within an organization feel there are specific actions and behaviors expected of them and when those actions and behaviors are framed in the context of doing, engagement evolves—engagement that integrates accomplishment and emotional satisfaction.

Engagement is not an elusive, indescribable, and immeasurable quality. Having studied its characteristics extensively, we have identified eight tenets that thoroughly define engagement, described in behavioral terms. *Team members who are engaged*

1. demonstrate business acumen,
2. use continuous improvement tools,
3. show accountability through actions,
4. take ownership for personal development,
5. demonstrate altruistic decision making,
6. perform collaborative mentoring and coaching,
7. are passionately self-motivated, and
8. demonstrate positive affirmation.

Assessment: "Acquiring" the engagement status of your team members

As you "fire up" your leadership GPS, the second "satellite" you must acquire is a fix on your organization's employee engagement. How engaged are your team members? This assessment will help you determine the level of engagement in your organization.

Instructions: Check off each statement that is true for you and/or your organization.

1. Team members don't think "accountability" is a "dirty word." Everyone accepts personal accountability for their work.

2. Everyone on the team is fully engaged; everyone is a "go-to" person.

3. The organization uses tools such as a business scorecard and an action register to hold everyone visibly accountable for working toward success.

4. Associates have the opportunity to influence goals before they are created.

5. Team members speak about their work and their goals with a sense of pride and passion.

6. Meetings are meaningful and focused on business-related issues. They are part of the business, not an addition to the business.

7. Meetings are considered a way to help achieve goals. They are not considered a waste of time.

8. Meetings start and end with a review of action-register items, which hold people accountable.

9. Every team member can tell you how his or her work relates to achieving overall company goals.

10. Associates work with a sense of urgency, accountability, and direction. They are engaged in the organization.

How many statements did you check off as true? Use this rating scale to measure your progress:

5 or fewer "true" answers—You are off course. Please recalculate.

6–7 "true" answers—Detour ahead. Calculate an alternative route.

8–10 "true" answers. You are on course. You will arrive at your destination.

This short assessment gives you a picture of the amount of employee engagement current in your organization. As you implement leadership GPS into your organization, revisit the assessment. Your goal should be to check off all of the statements as true.

CHAPTER 3

Do You Have Leadership Systems in Place?

Gabby—our car's GPS—needs to acquire signals from at least four satellites to get precise bearings of latitude, longitude, and altitude. Those signals tell her where she is, so that she can calculate how to get to where we want to go.

Leadership GPS needs to acquire the leadership locations from *three* "satellites": *goals, people,* and *systems.*

The Merriam-Webster dictionary defines "system" as "a regularly interacting or interdependent group of items forming a unified whole." The key words are *interacting* and *interdependent.* When several leadership systems interact and become interdependent, high-performance organizations that function with clarity, connectivity, and consistency result.

What are the systems that yield clarity, connectivity, and consistency? We have alluded to them in the previous two chapters:

- A Business Scorecard system
- An Accountability system
- A Communication system

Figure 3-1 Employees Don't Leave Jobs

We can't truly appreciate fully how these three systems work together to sustain business success until we understand how organizations traditionally *(mal)function* because they *don't* have these systems in place.

Managing by the 3 Ps

Leaders in today's complex economy are faced with a multitude of challenges, many of which you can relate to—acting as a coach, mentor, facilitator, mediator, educator, scheduler, HR person, and motivator, to name a few roles. They are asked to do more with less and yet motivate their teams to meet the organization's mission and goals. Today's leaders are pulled in so many directions that they are pulled *away* from their associates—the people with whom they should be most connected. Is it no wonder, then, that associates feel disengaged, since their leaders do not have time for them?

Faced with so much, how do most leaders get their work done? *The old-fashioned way*—managing by the three Ps—*position, proximity,* and *persuasion.* Unfortunately, managing by the 3 Ps is not very effective in the long term. Here's why:

Managing by position

Title and authority. Some people seek them because once they have title and authority, they feel powerful; people stand in awe of those who hold them.

Traditionally, leaders have used title and authority—"Do it because I said so!"—to achieve results. They set policy, give direction, and make decisions they expect others down the line from them will execute.

We respect title and authority. When leaders use them appropriately, title and authority get results. But leading by title and authority has a problem: If the leader goes away, the organization flounders. Organizations that depend upon title and authority to achieve results are sooner or later disappointed because a title alone cannot sustain success.

Only process and system can do that.

Fleeting success

Two friends were talking about their work situations. One of them lamented that nothing was going right. "Why is that?" his friend asked. "I thought your department was the sweetheart of the company, with all the success it was claiming."

"It was," replied the other fellow. "But a few weeks ago the vice president in charge of our department left. And now everything is in chaos. No one is starting another project, because they are waiting for the new boss to tell them what to do. They don't want to start something and have it squashed later. No one is making decisions. Everything seems to have ground to a halt. I just wish they would get their act together and hire someone soon."

This company was a classic case of management by position.

Managing by proximity

It's a natural phenomenon: People work more conscientiously when the boss is standing nearby. Do you doubt it? Think about the last time the CEO of your company paid your location a visit. Wasn't extra effort made to spruce up the facilities? To make sure everything was clean and painted? To put everything in its place?

But isn't your facility supposed to be kept clean *every day*—not just when a senior executive decides to pay a call?

A sign of proximity management

A manager tells this story: "We were communicating with a manager whose company's headquarters are in England. For several days, we tried calling and e-mailing the client; calls and e-mails went unanswered. Finally we heard from him. 'Sorry I haven't been in touch. The top brass from London are expected next week. You can imagine how hectic it's been around here!'"

Hectic, for sure—if management by proximity is the norm.

A visit from the CEO is an extreme example of managing by proximity. More commonly we call it MBWA—managing by walking around. Yes, it is important for the boss to walk around and see what is happening. But when walking around—being on the floor—is the *primary* way to make sure things get done, that is *managing by proximity*. The problem with this type of management? It cannot sustain itself, because the boss cannot be everywhere all the time. What happens when she goes on vacation or he attends an out of town meeting? Does the work get done? Do decisions get made? Or does everything remain in status quo until the boss returns? Where is the accountability?

Managing by persuasion

In the last 20 years, leaders have learned how to persuade employees to perform. They have been trained to ask, not tell, and to show employees what's in it for them in order to get them to do anything more than the minimum (and sometimes just the minimum!).

Persuasion works—in the short term (just like managing by position and proximity). But something is inherently wrong in the organization if a leader must *always* show associates how their work is connected to the organization's success. Something is lacking. Besides, managing by persuasion is a time-consuming endeavor. Who has time to dicker with every employee over every task? And what happens when the supervisor is not present to dangle a carrot? Does the work get done? Do corrective actions occur? It's very doubtful.

Even worse: When an organization is characterized by managing by persuasion, time-crunched supervisors tend to rely on their "go-to" people to get things done. They do this because they don't have to take the time to cajole and persuade, and they know the go-to people don't need to be convinced to do their work. To be sure, at least in the short term, the work gets done, but at the risk of burning out the real go-getters (and even the supervisor)—and at the cost of failing to engage the rest of the workforce.

Management by persuasion shortchanges the opportunity for success.

Can you relate to this?

Two supervisors were walking out of their weekly staff meeting. One said to the other, "So, the boss wants your team to make sure that new project gets done by next Tuesday. Who on your team do you think will take it on?"

"Who?" the other supervisor asked, in turn. "Who, indeed! Me, that's who. I'll do it," the colleague retorted dejectedly.

"But you don't have to," said his friend. "It's your team's responsibility to get it done, not yours personally. The boss doesn't expect you to do it yourself."

"Look," replied the other. "I've learned the hard way, 'If you want something done, do it yourself.' By the time I convince someone on my staff it has to be done, I could have finished it myself. Arguing over it just isn't worth the effort."

"But you already have a lot on your plate," said his friend. "You're going to burn yourself out if you're not careful."

"'Going to' burn myself out? Ha! I think I've already done that. I'm ready to throw in the towel."

And that's what can happen when an organization manages by persuasion.

Process Based Leadership Systems

What the 3 Ps do to an organization can be summed up in three words: *They create dependency*. Employees become dependent on their leaders to make the decisions, to solve the problems, to show them what to do and when to do it. Certainly managing by position, proximity, and persuasion gets short-term results. But dependency is dysfunctional. Leadership GPS breaks the cycle of dependency with its process-based leadership systems.

High-performing organizations need sustained results. To achieve this end, organizations need *process-based leadership systems* that are not dependent upon authority, presence, or an individual's gift of gab. In fact, when these systems are in place—*Business Scorecards, accountability,* and *communication*—whether the leader is present or not makes little difference. The organization—meaning the people within it—does what it needs to do to succeed. They become interdependent, responsibly relying on each other in a positive way.

Let's take a brief look at each of these three systems.

Business Scorecard

The first system that runs throughout and helps bind the leadership GPS process is the Business Scorecard. It connects people to the business.

The scorecard that our leadership GPS system utilizes is dynamic. Think of the scorecard in this way: Those used in other programs are static. Those scorecards tell the score, to be sure, but they don't do much else.

The Process Based Leadership® (PBL) Business Scorecard we use in leadership GPS is active. With a glance, it

BL ScoreCard®

ID	Objective		Target	Owner	Frequency For Review	July	August	September	YTD
	ScoreCard								
	Key Focus Area								
4246	SMART Objective Metric		100	Metric Owner	Monthly				
	Key Focus Area								
4249	SMART Objective Metric		100	Metric Owner	Monthly				
	Key Focus Area								
4252	SMART Objective Metric		100	Metric Owner	Monthly				
	Key Focus Area								
4255	SMART Objective Metric		100	Metric Owner	Monthly				

Figure 3-2 Scorecard

reports whether the organization is winning or losing in its goal achievement, and it can be adjusted accordingly. (Those adjustments are done through tools in the accountability system, such as the Action Register.)

As we mentioned earlier, business-focused scorecards are tools that are used to accomplish the following tasks:

- **Educate.** Because scorecards are developed around a set of key business areas (such as quality, safety, cost, productivity, people, and customer service), they create a common language that everyone in the organization learns and uses. Even an associate at the lowest level of the organization can look at the corporate scorecard and understand what it says.

- **Facilitate.** Weekly meetings in high-performing organizations are focused around the Business Scorecard, with teams discussing what went well during the last week and what did not go so well—and the corrective actions they need to take to get back on course.

- **Motivate.** Teams develop their own goals, objectives, and corrective action plans. They relish their accountability to achieve and take pride in celebrating when goals reach the "green" state.

When these things occur, people feel connected to the organization.

Business-focused scorecards → Connectivity

Accountability

In the previous chapters, we described the importance of business-focused goals and engaged people. And we gave examples of how goals work for an organization. You might have noticed one word surfacing innumerable times in those chapters — *accountability*.

In high-performing organizations, engaged team members take ownership of their work. They take ownership of the company's goals. And they hold themselves accountable to do their best — always. When they don't, consequences result. When they do, they celebrate success. (That's what accountability is all about: Accepting responsibility, risking consequences, enjoying rewards.)

Accountability is what we call a "nonnegotiable." High-performing organizations do not debate about whether someone should be accountable or not; they are accountable or they do not work for the organization. Accountability is a condition of employment in these organizations.

Of course, accountability doesn't just happen. It needs to be cultivated and interwoven throughout the various performance processes. It is not something that can be selectively chosen. It can't be "told" to employees.

Accountability as a system must be ever-present in all expectations for success, whether they relate to behavior or work performance. *(We will talk about how to develop and maintain accountability in a later chapter of this book.)*

When accountability is an accepted system of behavior in an organization, team members know they can depend on

31

their leaders as well as each other. They understand and accept expectations for how they behave and how they perform.

Accountability → consistency

Communication

The third system—*communication*—is intricately intertwined with Business Scorecards and accountability. It is through a real communication system—face-to-face two-way talk as well as tools that provide clarity of intent and action—that goals are developed, accepted, and achieved. It is through this same communication system that people affirm their accountability, from job performance to individual behavior.

In high-performing organizations, communication is a process that always needs improvement yet still gets rave reviews from associates. These organizations value and encourage true communication; they don't merely advertise.

We all know what advertising is—a marketing effort to encourage an audience to take action (usually to buy something). Most companies have great employee-oriented advertising programs—bulletin boards, intranets, newsletters, magazines, hot lines, memos, and e-mail—they pass off as communication. All of these programs serve a purpose—to inform. But don't be fooled: These media do not communicate. Communication, by definition, is a two-way process of sending and receiving messages—*face to face*.

In high-performing organizations, one of the key methods of communication is business-focused meetings. These are not ordinary meetings no one wants to attend. These are meetings whose primary purpose is to review the Business Scorecard, celebrate success, and discuss attainable corrective actions.

Weekly team meetings, one-on-one meetings between the team leader and individual team members, and town hall meetings with upper-level leaders are all examples of how face-to-face communication occurs in high-performing organizations.

When organizations implement a two-way communication system, policies, procedures, connection to the business, expectations—all become clear.

Communication → Clarity

The three Process Based Leadership systems—Business Scorecards, Accountability, and Communication—are so interwoven in leadership GPS it is often difficult to separate them. Consider the following example of a business based in Kansas.

Top down, bottom up

Every Monday morning, the top-level teams in the organization meet to review the scorecards submitted from the previous week *(Business Scorecards)*. The leaders discuss what went well and what needs to change *(Communication)*. They create corrective action plans *(Accountability)* on what needs to change, and cascade their scorecard down to the next level.

That level does the same, based on input from the top level, and cascades its scorecard down to the next level. By 3 p.m. on Monday afternoon all team members—from top to bottom—are aware of the status of the organization, what needs to be corrected, how it will be corrected, and who is accountable for reporting on the status of the correction. By the end of the week, all scorecards are sent up the line so that on Monday morning the process is repeated—using communication, accountability, and scorecards as systems to assure the sustainability of the organization.

Assessment: Do you have leadership systems in place?

The third "satellite" leadership GPS must acquire is Process Based Leadership systems. The following assessment will help you determine the current status of your organization's leadership systems.

Instructions: Check off each statement that describes you and/or your organization.

1. You find yourself having to monitor team members closely to make sure the work gets done.

2. Your to-do list contains tasks that someone else could have done, but it would take too much time to convince them to do it.

3. Whenever a new project comes down the line, you spend time explaining why it is important and what's in it for the team members.

4. You find yourself saying, "Do it!" more and more often. Your associates don't seem to take the initiative on anything.

5. You conduct team meetings, but people wander in late and sometimes not at all.

6. Only a few individuals participate in the team meetings.

7. You've heard people groan when you tell them about an upcoming meeting. They think of meetings as something to do in addition to their work.

8. If someone were to ask the status of a project, you would have to look it up.

9. The Business Scorecard posted in your break room hasn't been updated in weeks.

10. The scorecard is something sent down from "above."

11. Weeks after a problem has been addressed by your team, no one knows the status of the solution.

12. If something doesn't get done, it's not unusual to hear "It's not my job" from team members.

13. You have a only couple of associates who you would say are "go-to" people.

14. Communication in your company consists of memos, e-mails, the company intranet, a newsletter, and an annual facility-wide meeting with the CEO.

15. Meetings are seen as an addition to running the business, not part of the business.

How do you rate? In the previous two assessments you completed, the aim was to have a checkmark in each box. In this one, however, the aim is to have a clean slate—no checkmarks! Use the following rating system to check your progress toward adopting leadership GPS:

7 or more "true" answers—You are off course. Please adjust your settings.

4–6 "true" answers—Detour ahead. Calculate an alternative route.

3 or fewer "true" answers—You are on course. You will arrive at your destination successfully.

As you go forward with leadership GPS, take this assessment again with the goal of making each statement not apply to you and your organization.

SETTINGS

The next time you get ready to use your car's GPS, before you enter your destination, take a look at its settings. You may be surprised by what you find.

Settings for our car's GPS (Gabby) are found by clicking on the tools icon on the main screen. We discovered that by adjusting Gabby's settings, we can establish parameters for our trip. For example, we can decide to drive the most fuel-efficient route (even if it takes longer), or not to take toll roads, and to avoid ferries. In other words, by inputting the settings we desire for that trip, we affect how Gabby operates.

We set the boundaries for how Gabby processes information.

Our leadership GPS syem also has "settings" that establish parameters for the successful operation of our GPS. These settings help us deal with people — our associates and colleagues — so that we can create an environment in which accountability and subsequent engagement are par for the course.

In the next four chapters we'll take a look at each of these "people settings" so that leadership GPS can propel the organization toward sustained success.

Chapter 4: People Setting No. 1—Interpersonal Relations
Chapter 5: People Setting No. 2—Behavioral Expectations
Chapter 6: People Setting No. 3—Feedback
Chapter 7: People Setting No. 4—Leadership Traits

People Setting No. 1— Interpersonal Relations

Have you ever heard a frontline leader complain, "My job would be easy if it weren't for the people!" Maybe you've even made that remark yourself, in jest or in frustration.

Team members don't always do what you want them to do. They aren't always "motivated." They don't always listen. They sometimes fight among themselves. Maybe they also fight with you.

Some frontline leaders estimate that people problems take up 70% of their time! That's a lot of hours that could be spent making the business better—if only the people problems would go away!

It's probably easier to fix a malfunctioning machine than it is to fix people problems. That's because you can easily remove a bad gear or replace a worn bearing or even modify a design. You can change a machine, but you can't change people.

That doesn't mean they can't change, however. They just have to have the environment and the tools to *want* to change. How people get along with each other—you with your team members, your team members with you, and your team members with each other—has a lot to do with building a productive work environment.

Figure 4-1 Nonverbal Communication

Communication happens when two parties exchange information face to face. However, even the best communication efforts are, by nature, challenged, because no two people can bring the exact same experiences to the exchange process.

Think about the wide range of life experiences in your work group: Your associates come in all shapes and sizes, metaphorically speaking.

- Some may be of different ethnic or racial backgrounds — perhaps may even be immigrants — and appear to think and do things differently from other team members.

- Other people reporting to you may be as old as your parents or as young as your grandchildren.

• And each of your associates (you too!) uses a unique communication pattern reflective of innate wants and needs.

Culture, generation, communication styles—these differences benefit the organization, but they can challenge you because, by their nature, differences beget conflict and miscommunication.

Our choices of words, tonal inflections, nonverbal facial expressions, and gestures—all products of our upbringing, our personality, our heritage, our culture, and our experiences—affect how the messages we send are received and how the messages we receive are interpreted.

We cannot eliminate the effect of our experiences from our communication efforts. But we can harness their differences so that we can improve the communication environment.

The first people setting we make in the leadership GPS process addresses interpersonal relations, which include the following:

• Cultural diversity
• Generational diversity
• Communication styles
• Listening processes

Cultural Diversity

Culture is the collective set of behaviors, experiences, and beliefs shared by a particular social, ethnic, religious, racial, or age group.

In some parts of the country, it is not unusual for an organization to employ people from a dozen or more different cultures or countries. The shop floor may sound chaotic—a mixture of languages, accents, and inflections. Such diversity is good; it allows the company to tap into perspectives it might not have otherwise considered. This type of diversity strengthens an organization in the long term. It has been proven that organizations with cultural diversity enjoy greater profitability—a sound business reason to strive for such diversity.

However, when cultures mix, it is not unusual for supervisors to have to deal with conflicts arising out of the diversity. For example:

- **Time issues.** Different cultures perceive and mark time in different ways. In some cultures, being on time means coming in late. In other cultures, being on time means being at a meeting ahead of the appointed hour.

- **Gestures.** Nonverbal communication is an area in which conflict easily occurs. For example, in America, nodding means "yes." However, in the Middle East, nodding the head down indicates agreement, while nodding up means disagreement! Thumbs up (an A-OK sign to Americans) is a vulgarity to people from Iran, and the OK sign formed by making a circle with the thumb and forefinger in America refers to money in some countries. To those from the Middle East, it is considered rude to hand something to somebody with the left hand; to Indians, a belch is considered a compliment to the cook; and in Latin

America, strangers embrace. The differences in nonverbal communication are as diverse as the world's community. And those differences can lead to conflict based on miscommunication.

- **Humor.** In some cultures, jokes do not belong at work, and any attempt to include someone of that culture would be insulting. In other cultures, mild joking and camaraderie are important to the workplace. Through them, people satisfy a great social need. Smiles and laughing may not indicate enjoyment, depending upon the culture.

- **Eye contact.** In Eastern cultures especially, making eye contact is considered rude, yet in American culture good eye contact is expected in face-to-face communications.

- **Communication styles.** In some cultures, silence is golden, and at work, members of those cultures may not participate in discussions. In others, silence is to be avoided at all costs. Members of a culture that abhors silence may tend to dominate group discussions.

- **Touching.** People from some cultures are "touchers"— not in an inappropriate manner, perhaps just a slight touch on the shoulder or arm as they are talking. However, people from other cultures never touch; to do so would be considered intrusive.

- **Information processing.** In some cultures it is considered rude to challenge anyone in a leadership capacity. What can happen, then, is that an individual says she agrees and will do as asked, but she never follows through.

(For additional differences concerning time, gestures, eye contact, humor, and touching, see Appendix I: Cultural Differences.)

These are just a few differences, and *anyone*—coworkers or supervisors—not familiar with cultural innuendo may inadvertently use offensive behavior or become angry or irritated because an individual from a different culture did not understand a gesture or joke.

So what should you do to get the most out of cultural diversity? Here are a few steps you can take:

1. **Learn as much as you can.** Volumes have been written on cultural differences. Take the initiative to learn as much as you can about the cultural backgrounds of your team members—especially if they are immigrants. An excellent resource is *Kiss, Bow, or Shake Hands* by Terri Morrison and Wayne A. Conaway (Adams Media, July 2006). This book has been reissued several times over the years, and different editions address doing business with different cultures around the world in various settings. Another excellent resource is *Cultural Intelligence: A Guide to Working with People from Other Cultures*, by Brooks Peterson, Nicholas Brealey Publishing (January 2004)—which allows you to test your cultural intelligence and provides tips on how to improve it.

2. **Discuss differences with the team.** Everyone needs to understand behavioral expectations. Use culture as an opportunity to learn about other cultures and to discuss your expectations.

3. **Set clear expectations.** Cultural differences exist, but associates also need to know specifically what is expected of them—such as participating actively on teams. Use expectation setting as an opportunity to explore differences and highlight what needs to be done.

4. **Ask.** Not sure if what you said or did was offensive? Ask. Talk about these perceptions with the individual.

5. **Be respectful.** If you inadvertently offend someone from a different culture, apologize, explain what you meant, and move on.

6. **Focus on business.** Keep team members focused on their common goals, not on their differences. Use the team's Business Scorecard to keep everyone focused on what is important for the organization's success.

Generational Diversity

Twenty or 30 years ago, in a typical workplace, the "top boss" was almost always significantly older than employees he or she managed. The work group itself would be homogeneous with regard to age (usually gender too).

Not so today. Gone (with few specific exceptions) is mandatory retirement. And, because of the economy, many people of "normal" retirement age (65+) continue to work—often next to the newest hires, the youngest team members, 18 years old. The result is that in today's workforce we have four generations of people working side by side. That can create problems, because people are a product of the events and experiences they grew up with. What they lived through in their formative years affects their outlook on work, how they communicate with each other, and how they get along. A survey by human resources consultant Lee Hecht Harrison confirmed that generational differences affect the workplace: The study said that 60% of employers report experiencing intergenerational conflict!

Let's briefly look at each of the four groups—the Matures/ Traditionalists, Baby Boomers, Generation X, and the Millennials.

Matures/traditionalists

These are the individuals who are in their late 60s or older; they constitute less than 5% of the workforce today. Many of them would like to retire but cannot because of economics. Others continue to work because that is "what they do." Work fulfills them socially and gives them a sense of purpose.

Matures are rewarded each time they get their paycheck. They don't need much more recognition than that.

Matures are perceived as follows:

- **Hard-working and trustworthy.** They dig in and do the job they are given. They see motivation as a moral obligation.
- **Loyal.** They have stuck to a job and have not changed organizations often throughout their long career.
- **Economically conscientious.** They've been through recessions and have had to pull in their belts, so they try not to be wasteful.

- **Trusting of authority.** Matures were brought up on the idea that the boss was the boss. What he or she said was true. They learned to do what was asked of them. Consequently they prefer decisions to be driven from the top down.

- **Optimistic.** Because they have been through bad times, they've also seen good times emerge, so they maintain an optimistic attitude about the future.

- **Self-supporting.** If they are doing a good job, they don't need feedback.

- **Strongly moralistic.** They have a strong sense of ethics.

Matures take pride in saying, "I do things the right way." They are motivated because it is "the right thing to do."

Baby boomers

Baby boomers, approximately 39% of the workforce, are those who were born between 1946 and roughly 1966. The earliest-born boomers are now starting to retire—or wish they could retire, if only the economy would allow them to.

Throughout the prosperous times when baby boomers were being raised, a number of social changes occurred in the United States—such as the drug-influenced culture of the hippies, the leftist culture of the yippies, and the fun loving of the yuppies. These cultural changes left marks on boomers, who can be described as follows:

- **Lean toward being rebellious.** They question authority and challenge decisions made without their input. They expect some say in decisions.

- **Are driven by the pursuit of goals.** They like having something to work toward; it just makes sense to them. They are motivated by effecting change.
- **Put their careers first.** They are willing to put in time on the job because that gets them ahead.
- **Are open to alternatives.** Probably because they have lived through so much cultural change, they are open to new ideas.
- **Value time off.** They want to be able to take time away from work to recharge their batteries after they have worked hard.
- **Would prefer a traditional retirement plan with benefits.** They want what was promised to them when they were hired.

Because of the times in which they grew up, boomers like to say, "I can change anything."

Generation X

Born roughly between 1967 and 1987, gen Xers (about 32% of the workforce)—the MTV generation—were shaped by the political and social events of their youth. For example, in 1973, the United States experienced a severe oil crisis; gasoline was rationed, and gen Xers, who were then children, sat in cars with their parents, waiting in long lines to buy a few gallons of gas.

In 1986 the Chernobyl disaster occurred, and the space shuttle *Challenger* blew up. In 1987 the stock market crashed on Black Monday. It was during their youth, too, that the first home computers were introduced and technology exploded in the workplace.

Gen Xers can be described as follows:

- **Discouraged and disheartened.** Events took their toll on their outlook in life. They saw their parents lose jobs and struggle through recessions.
- **Good with technology.** They grew up with computers; they don't know how to do without them.
- **Clever and resourceful.** Perhaps because of technology, they are good at finding ways to do things differently. They are motivated by having flexible responsibilities and seeking status.
- **Determined and self-reliant.** They grew up as latchkey kids, with both parents working or as a product of divorce. They learned early to do for themselves and not rely on anyone else.
- **Loyal to people, not companies.** They have seen how recessions affected their parents.
- **Quick to change jobs when they are dissatisfied.** They don't complain; they leave. Since companies are quick to lay off, they feel no obligation to stick around if something better comes their way. They would prefer a portable 401(k) with lump-sum benefits for retirement.

Gen Xers like to say, "I work to live, not live to work."

Millennials

Born between approximately 1987 and 1998, this group (also known as generation Y) is the youngest we have in the workforce and constitutes about 25% of workers. They are the first to be "always connected" by technology. They don't know what it is like not to have a smart phone or a personal computer. They have been raised in an era of terrorism, which has tainted their outlook and trust of people. And many of them have entered the workforce during the time of the Great Recession, making it more difficult for them to find jobs and/or use their education.

Millennials—also known as generation Y—can be characterized as follows:

- **Are team-oriented.** They learned team behavior from socializing in groups, rather than traditional dating.

- **Do not trust easily.** Perhaps because they have seen so many promises broken, they always want to know "why" before they accept a decision.

- **Are good at multitasking.** They are the generation that had activities planned by their parents and learned to juggle school with sports and social events.

- **Respect titles and positions.** They want a relationship with their boss, but they also want flexibility to balance work and life.

- **Are resilient and realistic about their futures.** They are motivated by challenging and innovative work responsibilities.

- **Are well educated.** They have come into the workforce highly educated. And they want to keep learning.

- **Want to be given tasks and left alone.** At the same time, they want to know why a task is important before they begin.

- **Prefer collaboration in decision making.** They only want a little guidance from a team leader.

Millennials like to say, "There's more than one right way."

It's always dangerous to make assumptions, but in general we can say that each generation of workers has a different outlook on life and work. They want different things; they respond to authority differently. Those differences can create the potential for conflict.

For example, the following can be said of the four groups:

- **React differently to how they are managed and how decisions are made.** Matures, for example, accept authority. Baby boomers and gen Xers have a tendency to question and rebel. Millennials question "why" before they act.

- **Are motivated by different things.** Matures are motivated by the paycheck; baby boomers more by time off. Gen Xers and millennials value flexibility.

- **Communicate differently.** Matures grew up with face-to-face communication; they often do not use technology to stay in touch. Millennials, in comparison, communicate with 140 characters at a time as they Twitter. To them e-mail is passé.

- **Have different views of life and work.** Matures come in, do their job, and leave. They like the structure of a regular work day. They accept overtime as a way to be rewarded with more pay. Gen Xers and millennials, on the other hand, like time off. They work to be able to play. Millennials especially like a fun environment, with flexibility in when and how they work.

Motivating and managing the generations

When you manage a multigeneration workforce, you rapidly realize that each generation has its own needs and wants. Trying to address these various needs creates great inconsistencies, and that in turn, results in even more conflict.

What to do? Focus on what they all have *in common* — the business — helping the business win, not lose. They all have the following:

- **A need for being connected to the business.** When you eliminate all the differences, the one thing all of these generations (and cultures) have in common is the business. They all work for the same organization. Use that connection to your advantage; turn their attention to business performance.

- **A desire to show what they can accomplish.** Everyone wants to do his or her best. Direct those efforts to business success.

- **A need to have clarity and consistency in their lives.** Regardless of generation, everyone functions better when they know what to expect.

- **A desire for recognition and affirmation of a job well done.** Everyone wants to know that his or her efforts make a difference.

As a leader, you can use these common focal points to your advantage: Implement business processes that provide clarity, connectivity, and consistency. These business processes — systems — are addressed in the next chapters:

- Business Scorecards
- Accountability
- Communication

Communication Styles: D.A.R.E. to Understand

Understanding cultural and generational differences is important. Another way to improve communication—and interpersonal relationships—is to understand communication styles.

Psychologists, studying the way people interrelate, have found that people primarily communicate using one of four different basic communication styles. These styles go by a number of different names; we use D.A.R.E.—Driver, Analytic, Relater, and Expressive.

Figure 4-2 D.A.R.E.

One style is *not* better than another. Each of us usually has a dominant style, and although we use some of all four styles every day, we usually are more comfortable expressing ourselves in our dominant style. Effective communicators, however, acknowledge the various styles and try to adapt their style of communication to meet the situation. When styles of communication match, barriers are reduced and true communication follows.

As you learn about the characteristics that differentiate the four types of communication styles, keep in mind the following:

- One communication style is not better than another!
- Highly effective teams have members with each of the communication styles—and they take advantage of the strengths of each of these styles.
- A team leader can have any style of communication.

Let's take a look at the characteristics of each of the four D.A.R.E. styles: Driver, Analytic, Relater, and Expressive.

D—Driver

As the label implies, Drivers are results oriented. Often, the first question they ask begins with the word, "What." They want to know what is going on, what the matter might be, what's the objective, and what they can do to move the company and the team farther along the road to its destination. For this reason, they are likely to feel at ease taking charge.

Sometimes Drivers come on so strongly they put others off. They can become impatient with someone they perceive as wasting their time. They like to be efficient and to get things done—now. On the other hand, they don't like others to make decisions for them. If pressured, Drivers will attempt to sell their ideas or become argumentative.

The easiest way to interact with a Driver is to let him or her take charge. This can pay off because Drivers relish a competitive situation and like to win. The leader who wants to get the best performance from Drivers will find ways to allow them the freedom to do things their own way.

What would a Driver's office look like? Probably plain or dull, but organized. They have just what they need to get the job done.

When Drivers are angry, they may raise their voice and walk all over someone. They have a tendency to force their ideas onto people. But a Driver's anger usually does not last long. It tends to be quick and then be gone.

Some of a Driver's strengths are decision making, a goal orientation, and persistence. They do not back down from a challenge.

The Driver	
Strengths	**Weaknesses**
Confident	Demanding
Decisive	Short-tempered
Fact-focused	Stubborn
Results-focused	Doesn't admit fault
Goal setter	Poor listener
Persistent	Argumentative
Compulsively active	Bored with small talk
Action oriented	Gives advice tersely
Thrives on challenges	Impatient with emotions

A—Analytic

Individuals who are Analytics seek a lot of data, ask a lot of questions, and behave methodically and systematically. The first question one is likely to ask is, "How?"—"How does it work?" or "How can that be?"

Analytics dislike making errors and being unprepared; they are not very spontaneous. They react to pressure or tension by seeking more data and digging for more information. Because of this, providing lots of data and information is the best way to communicate with them. Analytics like to be measured by the amount of activity and busyness they generate that leads to results. They aren't as apt to get to the destination as quickly as a Driver because they take into consideration a lot of data. They should be allowed to make decisions at their own pace. Cornering or pressuring Analytics is not likely to be productive.

Analytics feel a need to save face. They hate to make an error, be wrong, or get caught without enough information. Look for ways to create a structure, framework, or track for Analytics to follow. They are concerned with being organized, having all the facts, and being careful before taking action. Their need is to be accurate; to be right, precise, orderly, and methodical; and to conform to standard operating procedures, rules, and historical ways of doing things. They typically have a slow reaction time and work more slowly and carefully than Drivers. They are perceived as serious, industrious, persistent, and exacting.

Usually, Analytics are task oriented, using facts and data. They tend to speak slowly and use their hands frequently. They often do not make direct eye contact, and they control their facial expressions. Others may see them as stuffy, indecisive, critical, picky, and moralistic. They are comfortable in positions in which they can check facts and figures and be sure they are right. They have neat, well-organized offices. In stressful situations, Analytics will do what they can to avoid conflict.

Analytics consider both the pros and the cons of a situation. They can see the long-term effects and look at all the options. Analytics are much better at planning than they are at executing. They are also very good at scheduling, but their follow-through may not be as good as that of another communication style. Analytics may sometimes appear negative, moody, or passive-aggressive. They tend to hold things in, carry grudges, be perfectionists, and be outwardly unemotional.

Analytics can also be highly critical at times. They may not believe something can be accomplished without the proof, and they may not think an idea is good unless they came up with it.

When Analytics get angry, they tend to shut down. They may stop talking and say something such as, "It can't be done." Analytics can stay angry a long time and can hold a grudge.

The Analytic	
Strengths	**Weaknesses**
Patient	Plans instead of does
Detail oriented	Indecisive
Process focused	Perfectionist
Scheduled	Critical
Looks at all angles	Moody
Cautious	Holds things in
Fact focused	Unsympathetic
Deliberate	Negative
Logical	Inflexible

R—Relater

Relaters like positive attention. They want to be helpful, and it's important to them to be warmly regarded. Their first question tends to be, "Why?" as in "Why are you so down today?"

They dislike any form of rejection, being treated impersonally, and uncaring or unfeeling attitudes. When the pressure is on and tension is mounting, they are likely to become silent and may withdraw from the action. The best way to deal with a Relater is to be supportive and show you care. Friends and close relationships are of paramount importance to the Relater.

A way for a leader to improve the productivity of a Relater is to provide structure and clear goals and to suggest ways and methods each goal might be achieved. It helps to be specific about plans and the activities to be accomplished.

Relaters need cooperation, personal security, and acceptance. They are uncomfortable with discord and try to avoid conflict at all costs. Some will sacrifice their personal desires to win approval from others. They prefer to work with other people in a team effort rather than individually, and they have an unhurried reaction time and little concern with influencing and making change. Typically, they are friendly, supportive, respectful, willing, dependable, and agreeable. Relaters react to stress by complying with others.

Relaters tend to use opinions rather than facts and data, to speak slowly and softly, and to use more vocal inflection than Drivers or Analytics. They may lean back while talking and do not make direct eye contact. They also have a casual posture and an animated expression. They may be perceived by individuals with other communication styles as conforming, unsure, pliable, dependent, and awkward. Their offices are likely to be "homey." Family photographs will probably be present in abundance, and there are likely to be plants or other living things.

The Relater	
Strengths	**Weaknesses**
Pleasant	Indecisive
Easygoing	Avoids confrontation
Dependable	Not a risk taker
Mediator	Nondisciplinarian
Inoffensive	Worries too much
Nonjudgmental	Shy
Caring	Sarcastic
Well balanced	Does not push back
Calming	People pleaser

E—Expressive

Expressives tend to get excited easily and may be excited most of the time. Their first question is likely to be of a personal nature, "Who?"

Expressives dislike long, boring explanations and can feel that time is wasted when the team dwells on too many facts and figures. They prefer to save time and effort by relying on hunches, intuition, and feelings.

When the pressure is on, they may react by trying to sell their ideas and can become argumentative. In stressful situations, Expressives may resort to personal attacks.

The best way to interact with Expressives is to mimic their style. Become excited right along with them. Show emotion. Expressives like applause, feedback, and recognition.

They embrace challenges and move ahead quickly. A leader is wise to provide some structure and plenty of recognition to Expressives. The best results will come by inspiring them to attain bigger and better accomplishments.

Expressives enjoy involvement, excitement, and interpersonal action. They are sociable, stimulating, enthusiastic, and good at involving and motivating others. They are also idea people. They can have little concern for routine, are future oriented, and usually react quickly. They need to be accepted by others; tend to be spontaneous, outgoing, energetic, and friendly; and are focused on people rather than tasks. Typically, they use opinions and stories rather than facts and data. They speak and act quickly, vary vocal inflection, lean forward, point, and make direct eye contact.

They use their hands when speaking, and they have a relaxed body posture and an animated expression. Their feelings often show in their faces. They are often perceived as excitable, impulsive, undisciplined, dramatic, manipulative, ambitious, overly reactive, and egotistical. They usually have unorganized offices and are likely to have golf clubs or tennis racquets and such hanging about.

The Expressive	
Strengths	Weaknesses
Friendly	Talks a lot
Motivating	Interrupts
Embraces change	Forgetful

The Expressive	
Strengths	**Weaknesses**
Humorous	Undisciplined
Generates enthusiasm	Easily distracted
Curious	Takes feedback personally
Creative	Unreasonable under pressure
Spontaneous	Has emotional highs and lows
Optimistic	Thoughtless

Labeling and understanding your communication style is important. What's important to understand, however, is that you can flex your communication style to match another's as the situation calls for. Everyone can learn how to adapt his or her style and be a more accommodating communicator. The more adept a person is at flexing styles, the more easily he or she will be able to communicate.

Listening Processes — *Really* Listening

The "people settings" in leadership GPS require more than just learning about what gets in the way of effective communication (and interpersonal relationships). They require doing something about removing the barriers—taking active steps to put into place good communication skills so that the rest of leadership GPS can flow without mishap.

In this chapter we've looked at cultural, generational, and individual differences in communication. Now let's look at what *you* can do to minimize those differences.

In a nutshell, listen. *Listen actively.*

An active listener shows that he or she is a full participant (*that is, engaged*) in the communication process. An active listener doesn't just react to the sounds someone makes (that's hearing), but instead processes information from the sound (and sights—nonverbal communication) and does this in such a way that miscommunication is unlikely.

Here are the basic steps to develop the skills of an active listener:

1. **Pay attention.** Communication occurs in a cycle: You are both a sender and a receiver. Whichever role you are in, pay keen attention to the other person. Show your interest. You can do this by using good eye contact (but not staring); focusing on what the person is saying; not being distracted by what is going on around you; watching and responding to the other person's body language; and refraining from engaging in side conversations.

2. **Give feedback.** As you receive information, show that you are processing it. For example, paraphrase what the other person says. Paraphrasing, in the manner of saying "What I hear you saying is . . ." indicates not only that you are listening but that you understand what the other is saying.

   Another way to give feedback is to clarify as the conversation proceeds. Asking questions is helpful, such as, "What do you mean when you say …"

   And a third way to give feedback is to occasionally summarize the speaker's comments. "Let me sum up what we've been talking about. You said …"

3. **Show that you are actively listening.** Occasionally nod, smile, and use genuine facial expressions. Make sure your

posture is open and inviting. And encourage the speaker to continue with short comments, such as "I see . . ."

4. **Don't interrupt.** This might be the most difficult communication habit to change! When you interrupt, you allow your own thoughts and arguments to intercede. Interrupting is disrespectful of the other person. Let the other person finish, even if you don't agree.

5. **Respond in an appropriate manner.** Don't attack the other person, even if you disagree. Don't get emotional. Avoid name-calling and labeling if your opinion is different from the speaker's. Treat the other person with respect and dignity. You can do this, and even confront others, by being open and honest, and above all, employing the Golden Rule.

Assessment: How well do you listen?

Rate yourself on each of the following statements, using a scale of 1–5:

    1 = Almost never
    2 = Seldom
    3 = Occasionally
    4 = Usually
    5 = Almost always

1. I speak clearly and distinctly.

2. I match communication styles, flexing my style to match the person with whom I am speaking.

3. I don't speak in a monotone. I try to use expressive language and tones.

4. When I am given instructions, I repeat them back in my own words to show that I understand.

5. When someone talks to me, I give her my full attention. I do not text, answer my phone, or use my computer.

6. When I am in an intense conversation, I often paraphrase what the other person is saying, to make sure I understand.

7. When someone gives me some information, I clarify what he wants me to do with it.

8. Even in a heated argument, I allow the other person her say; I avoid interrupting to get my point across.

9. As I talk with someone, I watch that person's body language to make sure it is saying the same thing as the words I hear.

10. I often ask questions when I am having a conversation.

You should strive for a 4 or 5 as a rating for each of these statements. Is your perception of your communication skills the same as those your team members have? Ask them to complete this assessment anonymously. Compare the averages of their scores with yours. Work toward earning a 5 for each statement.

CHAPTER 5

People Setting No. 2— Behavioral Expectations

The next critical people setting concerns behavioral expectations.

You know your team members don't always behave as you would like them to. For example, some team members

- show up late to meetings,
- don't participate in discussions,
- turn reports and other assignments in late
- pick arguments with coworkers,
- take extra-long lunch hours,
- arrive late,
- leave early, or
- ignore using safety procedures.

The list goes on.

The truth be told—it's possible *you* don't always behave in ways your associates would like you to either! Perhaps, for example, you

- keep your door closed,
- limit your accessibility,
- micromanage,
- answer phone calls when you are in conference with them,
- keep information from the team,
- don't process performance reviews on time, or
- aren't prompt in processing vacation requests.

Some of the "misbehaving" may be caused by miscommunication. Hopefully, the first people setting—interpersonal relations—will address those instances. But, another type of miscommunication frequently occurs—miscommunication because of misunderstood behavioral expectations.

Let's clarify what we mean by "expectation."

An expectation, in its simplest definition, is an anticipated desired outcome. Sounds simple enough, but, unfortunately, expectations are usually built on assumptions, and since individuals call upon different sets of assumptions (drawn from their individual life experiences), expectations get muddied.

What is a clean desk?

A supervisor had one strict rule for her team: At the end of the day, everyone's desk should be clean. She felt her reasoning was sound: She did not want sensitive documents lying about, nor did she want to risk having information accidentally misplaced. She emphasizes this rule to every new person she hires.

She was surprised, then, when she saw that her newest team member was ignoring her rule. To her, the desk was a mess, loaded with stacks of paper and files. The supervisor addressed the problem with the associate:

"I thought I made it clear that your desk was to be cleaned off at the end of every day," she said.

The employee looked at his desk and replied, "Well, yes. And I cleaned it off."

"That's clean?" retorted the supervisor. "Clean means nothing on the desk."

The associate hung his head and replied, "Oh. I thought 'clean' meant neat and orderly, things in stacks and folders, which is how I left my desk. But now that I understand what you mean, I'll put everything away at night."

The root cause of almost all conflict is unclear expectations. Often, these conflicts (unclear expectations) occur because the statements we make are not action based. In the foregoing anecdote, to clarify her expectations, all the supervisor had to do was to say, "I want the desk to be clear of all papers and folders. You should lock up all files every night."

If you want your expectations to be met, you must clearly define and communicate them—not rely on assumptions. The best way to define expectations is in terms of the behaviors

The root cause of almost all conflict is unclear expectations between manager and employee. If you want expectations to be met, clearly define and communicate them.

Figure 5-1 Define Expectations

you can observe. When expectations are defined in observable terms, the chance for miscommunication diminishes.

In leadership GPS some behavioral expectations are nonnegotiable; others can—and should—be developed and agreed upon by the team.

Nonnegotiable Expectations

Nonnegotiables are the minimum processes that leaders and work groups perform to maintain focus, consistency, and accountability. As the name implies, they are not up for negotiation. They are, if you will, a condition of employment. And—very important—nonnegotiables apply to *everyone*—no exceptions—top leaders on down.

We recommend several nonnegotiable "settings" for organizations embracing leadership GPS:

- Accountability is everyone's responsibility.
- Everyone will participate in a weekly team meeting.
- We will use and update the business scorecard each week.
- We will use the Action Register to keep our business on track.
- We will treat one another with respect and dignity.

These nonnegotiables establish minimum standards for performance and behavior. They form the cornerstone of leadership GPS. Nonnegotiables provide you with a framework to give your organization habit, discipline, and structure, which in turn create and sustain a sense of urgency, a clear and concise business focus, and a sense of collective accountability.

Negotiable Expectations

When we talk about negotiable behavioral expectations, we are not suggesting that every exchange between you and an associate become a negotiation! Rather, negotiable behavioral expectations are agreed-upon ways for both team members and the team leader to behave in the workplace. These expectations apply both to leaders as well as to team members, but unlike nonnegotiables, which extend throughout the entire organization, negotiable behavioral expectations are team specific. The team and team leader develop and manage them. In other words, they negotiate what these behaviors are.

Negotiable behavioral expectations are important to the smooth operation of the work group. They define the behaviors that team members use to make sure the team operates effectively and achieves its scorecard metrics. They are team rules.

The negotiation process consists of three steps:

1. The leader defines in behavioral terms what he or she expects of the team.
2. The team members define, in behavioral terms, what they expect of the leader.
3. The team members define what they expect from each other.

After they agree on these three areas, the team must do one more thing: decide on a method to deal with expectation violators. We've found that many teams decide to use a three-step method:

1. **One-on-one feedback.** The two individuals involved in a dispute over expectations engage in a direct effort to resolve the issue. In most situations, this type of confrontation resolves the issue immediately.
2. **Team discussion.** If one-on-one feedback does not resolve the issue, the issue is brought before the team by both parties, and the team resolves it.

3.   **Team leader meeting.** If the behavior continues, the team leader becomes involved by working with the individuals and reaching a final decision on how to resolve the issue.

Because work groups are fluid and things change, the team can (and should) review their negotiable behavioral expectations periodically and eliminate or update them as needed.

This people setting is a proven way to improve interpersonal relations and reduce workplace conflicts.

CHAPTER 6

People Setting No. 3—Feedback

The third critical leadership GPS people setting is feedback.

Feedback is a good thing. Without feedback we would easily go off track and get lost. Gabby gives us constant feedback, both visually (showing if we deviate from the pink line on the map) and audibly ("recalculating!").

So, if feedback is such a good thing, why is it that few people like to give feedback to anyone else, and even fewer like to receive it? The answer, most likely, is because when people have given us feedback in the past, it has been done poorly and in an aggressive, confrontational manner that put us on the defensive. Since we don't like to receive it, we figure no one else does either, and consequently, we become very uncomfortable giving it.

Not all feedback is reliable

Recently, we took an auto trip to visit the Gulf Shores National Seashore in the Florida Panhandle. The road into the park is close to the gulf. As we navigated the highway, we occasionally looked down at Gabby and the pink trail we were supposed to be following. We were surprised to see that, according to the feedback we were getting from Gabby, we were driving in the gulf! The feedback, obviously, was incorrect; it was based on outdated information (old maps—a hurricane had changed the shoreline).

Gabby is not perfect, nor are the people you work with. Misconceptions and misunderstandings can occur, so feedback is not always correct or reliable. Nevertheless, always listen and thank the individual for taking the time to give you feedback.

Giving and receiving feedback do not have to be uncomfortable. Learning the feedback process is important to our interpersonal relationships in the workplace, because as leaders we must give feedback. And we must also be able to receive feedback so that we can continue to grow and contribute to our organization's success.

We recommend a simple process for *giving* feedback: the SBI model—state the situation, behavior, and impact. This model focuses on the situation not the individual, so it takes personality out of the equation.

Example of SBI feedback

A member of your team has been taking long lunch hours, and this has been having an adverse effect on the rest of the team. Sometimes they have to pick up the slack, and they don't think that is fair. According to the team rules concerning behavioral expectations, one team member, Tom, confronts Mary with feedback:

Tom: "Mary, several of us have noticed that you have been taking 90-minute lunches all week. When you take long lunch hours, it puts an extra burden on us."

Mary: "I'm sorry, Tom. I should have said something to the team and made arrangements ahead of time. My parents are moving here and they needed me to help them this week. I apologize. It won't happen again."

Consider the following when you give feedback:

1. **Be aware of the individual's communication style and adjust accordingly.** For example, if the person is a Driver, get to the point immediately. If she is an Expressive, spend time on small talk.

2. **Give the feedback in private.** Don't pounce on the individual at the water cooler or copy machine. Find a private place to talk.

3. **Be specific.** Specificity is important. The individual cannot change a behavior unless he understands what needs to change. Use the SBI model.

4. **Do it in a timely manner.** Don't delay more than 24 to 48 hours. Any later, and the individual may not recall the behavior.

5. **Focus on the situation, not the person.** Stick to the facts.

6.   **Allow for two-way communication**. Hopefully the individual receiving feedback will not be defensive. Regardless, however, be prepared to listen.

Receiving feedback is no more fun than giving it, and in some ways, it is more difficult. Consider the following when you receive feedback:

1.   **Listen.** Don't interrupt; don't argue; and don't get defensive. Just listen to what the individual has to say, focusing on the facts, not the person giving the feedback. Remember that it is difficult for that person to confront you.

2.   **Do not attempt to justify your behavior.** Once the individual has given all the facts, you may want to offer an explanation. However, do *not* try to justify, such as, "I know I have been taking long lunch hours, but so has Jerry and no one said anything to him."

3.   **Be aware of the sender's communication style.** Adapt as necessary to improve the exchange between the two of you.

4.   **Clarify what you heard.** Paraphrase what the individual said to you to make sure you understood correctly. For example, "If I heard you correctly, you said I seemed to be taking long lunch hours."

5.   **Thank the person for providing the feedback**. Feedback is an opportunity to grow, and you should feel grateful for any such opportunity.

CHAPTER 7

People Setting No. 4— Leadership Traits

T he last setting we have to make is very personal, and it is very important, because it establishes the environment in which employee engagement can flourish. The setting deals with enhancing your leadership style.

Leadership GPS is about implementing processes and systems, to be sure. But it is more than that. To develop and maintain an effective workforce, the leaders within the organization must also manifest high-performing leadership qualities.

In Chapter 3, we briefly examined how typical organizations manage—through *power, persuasion,* and *proximity* (the 3 Ps). We found that managing by the 3 Ps promotes a culture of *dependency* on individual leaders. This dependency is, for the most part, dysfunctional.

Leaders who manage through the 3 Ps often get results— mainly due to their strong personalities. *They* set the direction; *they* determine how to reach goals; *they* take control of all aspects of running the business. With their superegos, these 3 P leaders swoop in and save the day! Saving the organization makes them feel good but unfortunately does nothing for setting a foundation for long-term success. This type of leadership drives loyalty to the personality of the leader, not a commitment to the business. (It is not unusual for a charismatic leader to "take" subordinates with him when he leaves an organization—and where does that leave the organization?)

Process-Based Leadership® is the opposite. Rather than encouraging dependency on the leader, it cultivates *interdependency*, in which team members are mutually and responsibly dependent upon each other. This is a good thing! As they become interdependent, they become more engaged. They care for each other; they watch out for each other; they help each other succeed. In a business setting, associates watch out for the interests of the company; the leader (as an agent of the company) watches out for the interests of employees. And this watching out is genuine and authentic.

Interdependency stems from leadership behavior. Managing through process allows the organization—your team members—to emerge from dysfunctional 3 P mentality.

Organizations today do not need larger-than-life saviors (3 P leaders) with magnetic personalities to drive performance. They need consistency and stable concentration on business focus, urgency, and accountability. Process gives these things; organizations that yearn to be successful need process-based leaders.

Managing through process means *you* (the leader) may have to make changes in your leadership style and adopt traits that encourage engagement and self-motivation. It may mean that you will have to learn to lead through your heart.

Make no mistake: True leaders have heart.

What is a heart-centric leader?

Heart-centric leaders channel their ego away from themselves and into the larger and more important goal of building a great team. That's because these leaders know (*really* know!) that success comes from the people; the leader is only a conductor who helps in the orchestration.

Heart-centric leaders are human beings, of course. They have egos and self-interest, and most are incredibly ambitious — but their ambitions are not self-centered; they are centered on the team's efforts and success, not their own.

Many books have been written on the characteristics and traits of effective leaders. All are worth emulating. But, as anyone who has attempted to fulfill New Year's resolutions knows, trying to change many behaviors at one time is overwhelming. What to do? We have selected five traits — a manageable number — that we feel most eloquently complement the leadership GPS process, and we suggest that you concentrate on incorporating them into your leadership style.

Figure 7-1 Servant Leadership

An effective leader—that is, one who has heart—cultivates these five traits:

- Humility
- Passion
- Stewardship
- Vision
- Integrity

Let's look at each of these more closely.

Humility

"Humility" is an often misunderstood term. Some people interpret "humility" to mean that a person must never say good things about himself, must never express pride in his work, and must always defer to others.

Nothing could be further from the truth. A humble leader is one who has a good sense of self—both strengths and weaknesses (limitations).

A humble leader.

- **Is unpretentious and modest.** He believes he is no better than anyone else. He is genuine, in a heartfelt way. And he never seeks hero or celebrity status.
- **Has a deep sense of self-awareness, not self-importance.** Self-awareness and self-importance sound similar, but they are complete opposites.

A *self-important* leader uses many "I" statements, such as "I did ...", "I accomplished ...", or "I solved ..." He really believes that an event or accomplishment occurred only because of him! And when he uses these types of statements, he shows a complete disregard for the input of others—their contributions, intelligence, knowledge, and skills. If you have ever heard employees talk about a supervisor who takes credit for their work, you can be sure they are talking about a self-important person.

A *self-aware* leader, on the other hand, intimately knows his strengths *and* his weaknesses. And he is aware that he has limitations. He seeks to eliminate or at least minimize weaknesses. Although he is deeply aware that he will never be perfect, he strives to improve. To that end, he seeks out feedback without becoming defensive.

- **Stands up for his beliefs.** When faced with a decision that might compromise his values, a humble leader is guided by a moral compass, which is often a simple question, such as "Would I want this on my epitaph?" or "Would I tell this to my son or daughter?" The moral compass allows the leader to check his motives before acting.

- **Is not jealous or envious.** Instead, a heart-centric, humble leader glows in the accomplishments of others. He channels his ego away from himself and into the larger goal of building an effective organization. His greatest personal satisfaction comes from watching his associates accomplish what they have set out to do— both personally as well as professionally.

- **Does not need to be first.** Leaders lead, right? Yes, but they do not always have to be first in line or see to their own needs before those of their associates. For example, a humble leader will often scorn the use of a private parking place, and would never consider cutting in front of anybody in a lunch line. A 3 P leader might do that, however, thinking his time was much more valuable than anybody else's.

- **Strives for win–win solutions.** A humble leader strives to mediate conflict, find common ground, and resolve differences. He knows that decisions made from an authoritarian position are rarely embraced, so he seeks collaboration and compromise and find a winning solution for everyone.

- **Is at peace with himself.** At the end of the day, a humble leader can sleep well, knowing that he has "done the next right thing."

Employees who work with a humble leader believe him, trust him, and respect him, because they know he has the business and their well-being at heart.

Passion

Passion has a place at work, in the heart of leaders (and associates). Passion helps drive success.

A *passionate leader*:

- **Doesn't let go.** She has a fierce resolve toward life, people, work, and the community. She wants the best and is not satisfied until she gets it.

- **Is relentless.** She doesn't stop seeking the best for her team and the organization. Her drive, however, does not originate from a need to satisfy her ego. Rather, it comes from a need to make her team flourish and the people on the team to grow and mature.

- **Is not complacent.** A passionate leader is never satisfied with the status quo. She believes she can learn something new each day and attempts to do so. She is intensely curious and is not satisfied until she understands the things that are unclear to her.

- **Is inspirational.** A passionate leader may be a Driver, an Analytic, a Relater, or an Expressive. Regardless of her communication style, however, she is a leader who inspires. She does not rely on theatrics to excite her associates. Instead, she has learned to share stories, often about herself and her life experiences, including mistakes she has made and lessons she has learned. Authentic sharing serves to inspire.

- **Surrounds herself with talent.** Egocentric (3 P) leaders who lack a sense of self often feel threatened by subordinates and peers who are smart, knowledgeable, and effective. But a humble, passionate leader knows better. She surrounds herself with people who are smarter and more clever than she is, because she knows that the sum is greater than the parts.

Employees who work for a passionate leader want to follow that leader and share in that leader's experiences. The leader's passion is so genuine it is contagious.

Stewardship

Stewardship is assuming personal responsibility for taking care of something that is not your own. A heart-centric leader is a steward of his organization. He is entrusted with serving the needs of the organizations and his associates. In other words, he does not take on the leadership role to make himself feel good (that is, to fulfill his own needs); he takes it on to fulfill the needs of those around him. He does not take over the responsibilities of others. Instead, he assumes the responsibility to make sure others succeed.

A *leader who is a good steward*:

- **Treats his associates as his best customers.** Just as a good server in a fine-dining restaurant anticipates the wants and needs of the diner, a leader who is a good steward anticipates and accommodates the needs of his associates, making sure they have the tools, skills, knowledge, and equipment (and the empowerment) to do the business of the company. He also anticipates and fulfills the needs of the business by envisioning the future, planning, and strategizing how to make the company successful. To this leader, the company and its associates are his customers.

- **Shepherds the character of his employees.** Self-centered 3 P leaders take care of their own needs over those of anybody else. They focus on "What's in it for me?" A heart-centric leader, on the other hand, asks, "How can I help make the business more successful?" That sometimes means reining in the tendency of employees to satisfy their own needs at the expense of the company. One way he does this is by holding his associates accountable. Building accountability in associates molds their character and at the same time helps focus them on the organization's success.

- **Knows what's important to his team.** A leader who is a steward to his team knows what is important to each team member. He knows this because he talks to each person, and he listens as they talk about their lives, their families, their goals, their activities—the drivers in their lives. He shows genuine interest in his associates.

- **Teaches his team to be self-sufficient.** A heart-centric leader teaches his associates to be self-sufficient, because in this way they will be able to succeed even when he is not there. He teaches self-sufficiency by putting into place processes and by holding them accountable.

- **Allows failure to happen.** No one learns until he *needs* to learn—in other words, no pain, no gain. Although a steward protects his people, he does not save them from learning experiences. He understands that failure (pain) is a way in which learning occurs. When his team fails, he does not place blame; rather, he helps his associates see how to avoid the failure the next time around.

Employees who have a leader who serves as their steward know they can trust him, and through that trust, they learn to accept responsibility and to grow to their fullest potential.

Vision

A heart-centric leader is one who has a clear vision for the future—and then shares that vision with her team and inspires them to make it real.

A *leader who has vision:*

- **Acknowledges reality.** The first step in solving any problem is to recognize it for what it is. A visionary leader takes a look at the culture of her organization and sees it for what it is—and if it is based on the 3 Ps as described in Chapter 3, changes it using leadership GPS.

- **Is able to tell a story.** Stories have three components: *Yesterday* ("where we came from"), *today* ("why we are here and how it feels"), and *tomorrow* ("where we are going and why I need you to go with me"). A visionary leader does not have to be a dynamic storyteller; she just needs to tell the story from the perspective of someone who is on a journey and believes that the journey is best traveled with companions, not alone.

- **Is optimistic.** Vision requires optimism. When optimism prevails, adversity cannot have the last word. A visionary leader is able to convey, in the midst of complacency or tragedy, the belief that tomorrow will be better and that each person possesses the ability to succeed. She is able to point to a place in the future to ground her people on where they are going, so that personality, position, and persuasion do not take them in the wrong direction.

Employees who have the good fortune to work with a visionary leader want to go where that leader is going. And through the leader's eyes, they can see the "destination." The clarity of the leader's vision begets loyalty and commitment.

Integrity

Life comes with its share of adversity. How we deal with adversity is the measure of our integrity.

Ironically, however, another measure of integrity is how we deal with success. A 3 P leader who tastes success often believes he can do *anything* and sometimes even puts himself above the law (legal or moral) that applies to everyone else.

In all the books on leadership, the one trait that is consistently named is integrity. Of all the five traits we identify in heart-centric leaders, integrity is the one that binds them all together. It is the character trait that causes us to do the "next right thing." Integrity is the foundation of principled leadership.

A leader who has integrity:

- **Is ethical and honorable.** In difficult situations in which the "easy way out" is tempting, he does the right thing. He does not bow to pressure, but follows his heart, guided by that moral compass we discussed earlier.

- **Is uncorrupted.** When a database maintains its integrity, it is said to be uncorrupted. The same can apply to a leader. When a heart-centric leader maintains his integrity, he remains "pure"—true to his principles.

87

- **Understands the importance of straight talk.** Integrity is all about straight talk that clearly articulates the situation, behavior, and impact (SBI). This SBI-modeled straight talk gives leaders the ability to confront barriers head on. The heart-centric leader who is guided by integrity does not avoid confrontation and conflict. He deals with it with straight talk.

- **Keeps his promises.** When a person accepts a leadership role, he commits to doing right by the organization and his team. A heart-centric leader keeps that commitment, that sacred promise. He understands that when wealth is lost, *nothing* is lost. When health is lost, *something* is lost. But when character is lost, *everything* is lost.

People who work for a leader who has integrity always know where they stand and trust their leader to be consistent and clear in his expectations for performance and success.

We feel that these five traits are within the realm of any servant leader. Set your parameters accordingly so that the leadership GPS process can flourish.

Assessment: Do you have the traits of an effective leader?

Read the following 25 statements and rate yourself on the five key leadership traits, using the following scale:

    5 = I agree with this entirely.
    4 = I agree somewhat.
    3 = I neither agree nor disagree.

2 = I disagree somewhat.
1 = I disagree entirely.

1. My team members would say I appear genuine.

2. I rarely use "I" and "me." Usually I use "we" and "us."

3. Based on the decisions they see me making, my team members would say I have a moral compass.

4. I usually praise associates publicly.

5. I regularly let my boss know about the accomplishments of individual team members.

6. When I am wrong, I apologize, even if it is to one of my team members.

7. My team members would say that I really enjoy seeing them succeed.

8. My associates would say that I never take credit for their ideas.

9. When I talk about the work I do, a stranger listening in would say I really love my job.

10. I rarely take shortcuts just to get the work done. Doing it right is more important.

11. Even when things are going badly, I try to remain optimistic and engender that optimism in my team members.

12. I encourage my team members to try new things.

13. I try not to stick to the tried and true but to experiment so that we can do better.

14. I encourage my associates to share their ideas about how the (company, department) can grow and change.

15. My team members would say that they have the proper skills, knowledge, tools, and equipment to do their current jobs.

16. I sit down with each of my team members several times a year to find out what is   important to them.

17. When I talk with my associates about their future, I take steps to help them get what they want in their career.

18. I would like to advance to the next level in my career in order to influence the shape and future of the organization—not just to get more power.

19. My associates would say that I treat them as a great customer.

20. My team members would say I take a genuine interest in them, both personally and professionally.

21. The last time my team failed, I was not happy but we used the failure as a learning experience.

22. I would never tell my team members to fudge a report or to ignore a quality problem.

23. My associates would say that I always keep my promises.

24. My team members would tell you that I hold myself accountable to the same set of rules they have to follow.

25. My associates have never heard me lie.

No one is perfect, but your goal should be a "5" for each statement. Because our self-perceptions can be skewed, however, if you really want to find out what you need to improve to become a principled leader, ask your team members to complete this assessment anonymously. Address any statement that earned less than a "4" average.

WHERE TO?

n Section 1: Acquiring, we "acquired" information on our organization's goals, people, and systems to find out if they needed to be improved, so that we could put into place a leadership process that could bring our organization sustainable success.

In Section 2: Settings, we set our leadership GPS's parameters of how to deal with people so that we could engage them in the business.

With all the preliminaries completed, now it's time to get under way!

When we are preparing to take a trip and Gabby asks us, "Where to?" we input the name of the state, the city, and the street address. She then consults our settings, and within seconds delivers to us visual and audible guidance to take us where we want to go, within our defined parameters.

As we determine "Where to?" in this section, we will set our direction and get under way with a fully integrated leadership GPS process.

Chapter 8: Goals and the Business Scorecard

Chapter 9: People, the Scorecard, and Engagement

Chapter 10: Continuing Your "Trip" through Productive Meetings

CHAPTER 8

Goals and the Business Scorecard

Acquire "satellites" —*check.*

Select "settings" —*check.*

Now it's time to go! *But where are we going?*
We have to set a direction and destination —*our
goals* —and integrate them into our Business
Scorecard.

The ultimate aim of the leadership GPS process is to
guide our organization to the sustained success enjoyed by
other high-performing companies. Leadership GPS makes
sure this happens by utilizing a critical leadership system: the
balanced Business Scorecard.

Like goal setting, scorecards are nothing new. Businesses have been using them for years. But most scorecards
are static. They are like thermometers: They tell you the
"temperature" ("Are we winning or losing?") of the business's
goals, but that's all. And even worse, they are not consistent throughout the business. The accounting department
may use one scorecard with its specific metrics unrelated
to production. The production department may use metrics
different from quality —and so on. Keeping watch on these

scorecards, people (often only the leaders) presumably know the status of their particular organization, but not what's happening elsewhere in the company.

Leadership GPS uses a different type of balanced Business Scorecard throughout the entire organization—*the Process Based Leadership (PBL) Business Scorecard*. It is not just a piece of paper or spreadsheet; it is a dynamic business "thermostat" that allows you to make adjustments to the business as needed.

As a system that reaches down, across, and up throughout the organization—translating business strategy to business tactics—the leadership GPS Business Scorecard accomplishes six important things:

1. Establishes a common business language
2. Tracks business results
3. Drives accountability at all levels of the organization
4. Is used in the decision-making process
5. Establishes priorities that link to corporate objectives
6. Increases employee engagement by connecting everyone to the business

The goal of the Business Scorecard is to provide an integrated system that measures each work group's impact on the company's strategic goals and objectives, and links action plans that all of the work groups are taking to maintain or improve performance on their key measures. The PBL Scorecard ties everything together in a neat, easy-to-use package.

Let's take a closer look at what a basic leadership GPS Scorecard includes in its design and how it is used to achieve these results:

ID	Objective		Target	Owner	Frequency For Review	July	August	September	YTD
	ScoreCard								
	Key Focus Area								
4246	SMART Objective <u>Metric</u>		100	<u>Metric Owner</u>	Monthly				
	Key Focus Area								
4249	SMART Objective <u>Metric</u>		100	<u>Metric Owner</u>	Monthly				
	Key Focus Area								
4252	SMART Objective <u>Metric</u>		100	<u>Metric Owner</u>	Monthly				
	Key Focus Area								
4255	SMART Objective <u>Metric</u>		100	<u>Metric Owner</u>	Monthly				

Figure 8-1 Blank Business Scorecard

Key Business Focus Areas

Key Business Focus Areas (KBFAs) are the broad areas that affect *every* aspect of the business — from production to sales to support functions (such as human resources and accounting). They form the common grounds — the standards, if you will — that make your business operate successfully.

It is the function of the top-level executive team in the organization (such as CEOs and their immediate reports, or plant managers and their direct department heads) to identify the KBFAs for the organization. They do this by carefully analyzing a number of key inputs (KIs), such as the following:

- Company mission
- Corporate objectives
- Measurement framework
- Stakeholders
- Issues and opportunities (SWOT analysis: strengths, weaknesses, opportunities, threats)

SWOT analysis

SWOT stands for the following:

- Strengths
- Weaknesses

- Opportunities
- Threats

A comprehensive SWOT analysis addresses both internal and external strengths, weaknesses, opportunities, and threats in each of the KBIs.

The top-level team identifies between four and six KBFAs that are highly pertinent to its business, such as the following:

- Quality
- Cost
- Safety
- Productivity
- People
- Customer service

Identifying the KBFAs is critical, because KBFAs:

- **Are the foundation for a common business language.** They forge the link between the strategic goals set at the top of the organization and the tactical-deployment goals on the scorecards used throughout the organization. The scorecard developed by the top-level team serves as a template for the ones used throughout the company. The same language, anchored by KBFAs, appears on all scorecards:

- **Head up the goals of every other team's scorecard.** Every other team forms goals and objectives to support the same set of KBFAs.

- **Balance the scorecard.** The scorecard is not skewed in only one direction, such finance. KBFAs take into account all the KBFAs that affect the ultimate success of the organization: finance, customers, internal business processes, and learning/growth of human resources.

Each KBFA is listed on *each* scorecard that *cascades down the organization* for a consistent approach to goal setting and managing the organization. It is important to note that although KBFAs cascade down the organization, they do not necessarily all roll up! In other words, all teams and individuals on each team will have objectives for each KBFA (for example, quality), but they don't all have to be working on the same metric—and most likely will not. The goals, objectives, and metrics that each team selects will be unique to that team. The assumption is that if the organization aims to improve quality (for example), all improvements to quality will have a cumulative effect, even though the improvements may be made in different areas.

The scorecard that the top leaders create serves as the template for all other scorecards used in the organization.

Although the KBFAs may seem logical and stand out to you and your team, be prepared to begin an educational journey as you cascade your business scorecards down the organization. Some team members—especially those on support teams—may not see their connection to the KBFAs. This may be a new concept for them! They may protest, "I'm in accounting. How does quality affect me? How can we have a quality goal or a safety goal?" In reality, everyone *can and should* work toward improving the same KBFAs.

A sports analogy may help illustrate how KBFAs apply throughout the organization:

In baseball, the goal is to win the game—in fact, to win the most games throughout the season in order to play in and win the World Series. The game's scorecard tells the status of the game (winning or losing), but the score itself does not tell the coach (or the players) how to improve so that they can achieve their overall season's goal (World Series championship).

To improve the team, the coach must look at individual components that contribute to winning (the team's KBFAs) and then help individual players develop their skills within each of these components. For example, the coach may decide that the individual components (KBFAs) for the team are hitting, throwing, fielding, and running.

Every player is expected to be able to hit, throw, field, and run—to some extent. Obviously, some players have been hired because of their superb hitting abilities (think Babe Ruth). The primary goal of these players may be to improve their percentage of base hits per game, so they work hard on hitting. At the same time, they must also be able to run fast (to get on and/or steal bases), be able to size up defensive plays (field), and throw accurately.

But players whose talents are not in hitting still have to be able to hit well enough to get on base. So they may focus on just making contact with the ball and hitting bunts or line drives.

A pitcher concentrates on throwing (pitching). However, he must also be able to field (throw to first, second, or third) and even hit (if only by bunting) to get on base.

And so it goes, for each player on the team. Each—no matter his position—performs in each of the KBFAs. As everyone works toward improving skills in each of the team's KBFAs, the team improves as a whole.

To illustrate how KBFAs apply to all types of teams, let's look at the following chart, which lists the most common types of KBFAs selected by top management, with examples of how production, accounting, and human resources affect them:

Examples of How Teams Affect KBFAs			
KBFA	**Production**	**Accounting**	**Human Resources**
Quality	Reducing scrap	Reducing number of errors on OT calculations	Improving retention rate after 1-year-onboard date
	Decreasing defects	Ensuring accuracy of orders	Providing mentorship programs
Cost	Maintaining costs to previous year's budget	Paying invoices on time to avoid late charges and take advantage of prompt-pay discounts	Reducing cost to fill open positions

KBFA	Production	Accounting	Human Resources
	Reducing overhead	Improving PO process	Decreasing overhead cost
	Reducing overhead	Reducing overtime	Decreasing number of unplanned absences
Customers	Eliminating customer complaints on late deliveries	Ensuring that orders are processed in a timely manner	Decreasing number of days to fill open positions
	Increasing overall customer satisfaction rating	Ensuring 99.5% accuracy of all invoices	Increasing average employee survey scores
Productivity	Increasing output per person	Improving efficiency in ordering supplies	Providing online training opportunities
	Improving production efficiency	Taking advantage of bulk order opportunities	Increasing training hours per associate
Safety	Reducing lost-time accidents	Maintaining a passing 6 S score.	Reducing lost-time days
People	Cross training team members	Providing cross-training opportunities within accounting department	Achieving affirmative action goals

You can see that, although each team affects KBFAs in a different manner, they all contribute, and the cumulative effect is that top-level goals made for each KBFA will be achieved through tactical implementation.

In business, once your team members see how their jobs affect the organization's KBFAs, there will be no going back. They will embrace the accountability of having goals linked to overall KBFAs, and they will feel connected to the business.

A realization that came too late

A company undergoing restructuring made the difficult decision to close one of its small operations. The leaders decided to engage an outplacement firm to help transition the workers to other jobs.

The workers had specialized in jobs that were found only in that plant within their community. The outplacement specialist wanted the workers to see how they could apply their skills, knowledge, and abilities beyond what they had done in this plant and thereby contribute to other companies.

As she worked with the group, she kept asking "why." "Why did you do that in your job?" "Why was that important?" "Why did that help the company?"

Finally, the light bulb went off, and one by one, the workers said, "I did my job to help make the plant profitable!"

The realization gave the workers a new perspective. One, however, had the last word: "Maybe if someone had really shown me how important my job was in the first place, we wouldn't have to shut this place down."

Sad, but maybe true.

SMART Goals/Objectives

Goals give the Business Scorecard direction. They answer leadership GPS's question, "Where to?"

Some people call them goals, others, objectives, claiming there is a difference between a goal and an objective. (Perhaps there is; we don't want to quibble over definitions.) Regardless of the label you give them, goals and objectives distinguish themselves by having five SMART elements as follows:

- Specific
- Measurable
- Achievable
- Relevant
- Timely

The goals developed at the top-level tier of the organization are highly strategic in nature. As the goal-setting/Business Scorecard process cascades down the organization,

Figure 8-2 Goals Should Be

however, the goals and objectives become much more tactical. The difference? At the strategic level, the leaders look to the future and forecast what the organization must accomplish by certain dates—perhaps a year or five years in the future. At the tactical level, the leaders (and team members) look at how they will make those accomplishments happen.

Don't be surprised if your team comes up with a wide array of goals to set and measure. Discipline yourself, however, to limit the scorecard to the *two or three SMART goals or objectives per KBFA.* Each objective the team develops *must* support its KBFA to advance the business.

Once you have decided on goals and objectives, you must determine their metrics—the key performance indicators

(KPIs) that measure the objective's accomplishment. As you decide on metrics, consider the following:

- Will timely, cost effective, and accurate data be available to you to measure the objective?
- Will your team be able to take action based on the results as the objective is measured—in other words, will the team be able to impact and control the outcome?

If the answer to either of these questions is "no," pick another objective and metric. Don't worry: Your team has plenty from which to choose, such as metrics that measure day-to-day accomplishments, key issues, projects, business processes, regulatory compliance—even areas of failure! Try to include a good mix of several different types of metrics on the scorecard.

What is a good metric?

A good metric (measure of performance) has several characteristics:

- Pertinent to the business (advances it)
- Objective (so it can be measured)
- Forward-looking (again, to advance the business)
- Actionable
- Timely
- Affordable
- Credible

To give you an understanding of how goals and objectives support KBFAs, consider these examples of metrics that support five KBFAs—quality, cost, customers, productivity, and safety:

KBFA—Quality

Objective: Reduce the number of defects for Product X from 55 per month to 52 per month by the end of FY.

Objective: Decrease the percent of rework needed from 3% to 2% by end of FY.

KBFA: Cost

Objective: Maintain costs within ± 10% of FY *budg*et.

Objective: Reduce overhead to < 15% of total costs for FY.

KBFA: Customers

Objective: Achieve a "very satisfied" response average 95% of the time for FY.

Objective: Reduce average call waiting time from three minutes to two minutes by end of FY.

KBFA: Productivity

Objective: Increase output per person by 5% over that for FY.

Objective: Meet delivery schedule 98% of time during FY.

KBFA: Safety

Objective: Maintain zero lost-time accidents during FY.

Objective: Reduce OSHA recordable accidents from three per quarter to zero per quarter.

Each of these objectives meets the SMART criteria of being Specific, Measurable, Achievable, Relevant, and Timely. Each would be entered under its appropriate KBFA on the scorecard.

Target

In addition to providing space to document each SMART objective, the scorecard has a column to identify a specific target the team aims to hit, noted in the target column. If the team hits the target, it earns a green color coding for the period. If it fails, it earns red. (Some teams adopt yellow, which indicates the target is in the danger zone.)

Owner

The owner column ties individual accountability to the score-card. The owner of the metric on the scorecard is the person responsible for the corrective action. This annotation dismisses any ambiguity about who is responsible for reporting on the status of the metric.

Tracking frequency indicators

The tracking frequency indicators are columns listing when the metric will be updated. The first indicator shows how frequently the goal is to be reviewed (such as weekly). The second indicator is posted results. At the time of its update, the owner colors the column in with green (winning), red (losing), and (if the team chooses) yellow (in danger of losing), along with the actual metric for the frequency period. With this color-coded system, anyone looking at a scorecard objective can tell at a glance if the team is winning or losing at that metric.

Notes

The scorecard should include a notes section. This is the space where the owner notes circumstances affecting the metric, such as "Supplier was two days late in delivering raw materials."

These are the basic columns a leadership GPS scorecard should contain. Although you can prepare a paper scorecard template or one using a spreadsheet, we recommend using the leadership GPS software version of the scorecard (PBL Score-Card), *which integrates the scorecard system with the accountability system and communication system.*

Leadership GPS Business Scorecards are essential for capturing your organization's goals and transmitting them throughout the business. And in the process of doing that, something magical happens: As people learn if the team and business are winning or losing, they become engaged. And engagement results in sustainable business success.

Business-focused scorecards → Connectivity

Spreadsheets or electronic scorecards?

Few organizations today use paper scorecards; they are too cumbersome and time consuming. Many companies use spreadsheets to track results. Certainly a spreadsheet is an easier, faster method of keeping results up to date, compared with doing it manually on paper.

However, you might want to consider trading in your spreadsheet for the PBL ScoreCard used in leadership GPS. Recent studies have found the following:

- 94% of spreadsheets contain errors ("A critical review of the literature on spreadsheet errors," Decision Support Systems, June 2008).

- 57% of spreadsheet users have never received formal training (ClusterSeven Consulting, June 2011).

- 71% of spreadsheet users have no audit process to check for accuracy (ClusterSeven Consulting, June 2011).

To get a better understanding of the types of metrics teams may use, go to Appendix II.

CHAPTER 9

People, the Scorecard, and Engagement

The organization's goals are set; the Business Scorecard is filled out. Now all we have to do is tell the "drivers" to go.

The drivers in the leadership GPS process are our people. Like drivers of automobiles, our team members must be engaged in what they are doing—or less than desirable outcomes will result. In real life, a distracted (unengaged) driver can easily get into an accident and cause damage, ranging from a mere fender bender to a fatality. Much the same can occur if our employees are not engaged: Studies have shown that businesses having a workforce of highly engaged team members outperform their peers by as much as 28%. But companies whose employees have a low level of engagement experience a *decline* in operating income of more than 32% (2008 Towers Perrin Global Workforce Report).

In Chapter 5: People Setting No. 2—Behavioral Expectations, you learned that you can and should set both non-negotiable and negotiable expectations (team rules) for acceptable work-group behavior. In essence, as you worked with your team to establish these workplace behavior rules, you and they were setting norms concerning team-member engagement.

Industrial psychologists Robert R. Blake and Jane Srygley Mouton in 1981 published a classic study on how establishing and maintaining workplace norms affect workplace productivity (*Productivity: The Human Side*, AMACOM). The authors found that, when a new norm—that is, an unwritten and usually unspoken standard of behavior shared by a group—is created, it is very fragile. Without appropriate reinforcement, those adopting the norm can and will easily regress to old behaviors. Blake and Mouton's study is more than 40 years old, but it remains as true today as it was then.

Simply *telling* your associates they must be accountable (and therefore be more engaged) won't get you to your goals. However, the leadership GPS process provides you with tools to sustain the accountability norm. These tools are the Action Register and the Personal Action Register. That's what makes accountability visible and real. These accountability system tools reinforce the norms you established.

Accountability → consistency

Action Register

In the previous chapter, we described the elements on the leadership GPS Business Scorecard that addressed goals and goal setting. The electronic Business Scorecard we recommend using has another tab on it—Action Register. This is the

Action ID	Actions	Applies To	Responsibility	Target Date	Completion Date	Comments	Administration
417	·	ScoreCard	**Metric Owner**	Jan 31, 2014 Add To Calendar	Mark as Complete	☐ Comments	Edit History
419	·	ScoreCard	**Metric Owner**	Jan 31, 2014 Add To Calendar	Mark as Complete	☐ Comments	Edit History
421	·	ScoreCard	**Metric Owner**	Apr 30, 2014 Add To Calendar	Mark as Complete	☐ Comments	Edit History
423	·	ScoreCard	**manager** **ScoreCard**	Jun 30, 2014 Add To Calendar	Mark as Complete	☐ Comments	Edit History
425	·	ScoreCard	**manager** **ScoreCard**	Aug 21, 2014 Add To Calendar	Mark as Complete	☐ Comments	Edit History

Figure 9-1 Blank Action Register

action plan that must accompany every metric listed on the scorecard; it must be created to address every goal whose status is in the red zone.

The Action Register is the logical extension of the Business Scorecard. The scorecard focuses everyone on issues important to the success of the business. *But focus is not performance.* That's where the Action Register comes in. *Performance happens when people are held accountable to act on the objectives that support the business.*

The Action Register documents that accountability because on it appear assignments of tasks to specific individuals, dates for completion of the tasks, and the results.

You will notice the Action Register has a format similar to the scorecard. Here's a breakdown on what each column means:

- **Action.** This is an assigned task, aimed at moving the business forward or correcting a problem.

- **Applies to.** This column refers to a specific metric.

- **Responsibility.** The name in this column is the person who is assigned to do the task.

- **Target date.** This is the date when the action is to be completed.

- **Completion date.** This is the date when the action was actually completed.

- **Comments.** Similar to the scorecard, this column allows the responsible party to record any pertinent information, such as results or status of the action.

- **Administration.** This section records modifications to actions and displays the reasons for each modification as well as who was responsible for it.

We've used the word "accountability" numerous times throughout this book. Some people take issue with the word. They think that team members will be taken aback at being held accountable.

Not so! We've found that team members actually love the concept of accountability—provided that their leaders are held just as accountable as they are! The scorecard with its integrated Action Register does just that: It assigns accountability to the appropriate individual. And it all becomes public knowledge, thus eliminating ignorance as an excuse for nonaction.

Because the Action Register is reviewed twice in each weekly team meeting (as part of the communication process— covered in the next chapter), its value as an accountability tool cannot be regaled enough.

Personal Action Register

Another tool that drives accountability—and engagement—is the Personal Action Register.

This accountability system tool is especially good at stopping the dependency cycle we so often observe when we visit companies having low employee engagement. Dependency occurs when the supervisor takes it upon him- or herself to solve problems for employees.

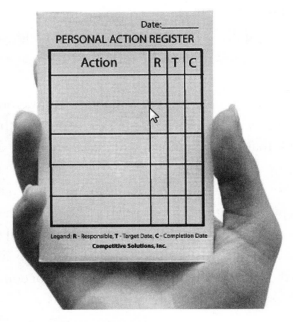

Figure 9-2 Personal Action Register

A sign of dependency

Recently we were taking a tour of a manufacturing plant with the plant manager, a well-liked individual. He carried with him a clipboard and pen, stopping often to talk with his people to find out how the job was going. Most employees chatted for a few minutes and went back to work. Some, however, eagerly waited for him and pounced on him with requests. One, for example, said, "I think I was shorted overtime on my paycheck last week." The employee pulled out the paycheck stub and handed it to the plant manager.

The plant manager took the stub, made a note on his clipboard, and said, "I'll look into it and get back to you later today."

That scene demonstrated a culture of dependency—that *management* would take care of problems. In a culture in which team members are fully engaged, the team member would take care of the paycheck problem himself.

For a long while leadership experts believed that a good manager "did" for his people. He solved the problems so that they could do the work.

Unfortunately, this type of management system creates dependency and stifles innovation, creativity, and initiative. It also burns out managers, who become overloaded with a myriad of tasks that detract from the real work—contributing to the success of the company.

We *all* want our associates to be paid the right amount. We want them to enjoy the full amount of vacation coming to them. We don't want them to be distracted by worries that take their attention off their business at hand.

But, if you have 15 associates and each has a "problem" that needs to be solved, you have just taken on a heavy burden if you decide to be the problem solver. Think of it this way: Although it might take only 10 minutes to find the solution to the problem, that's 150 total minutes—2 1/2 hours—added to your day if everyone asked you for something in one day! What could you do with 2 1/2 more hours to contribute to your organization's success?

The solution to this dependency problem is simple: Expect your team members to do what they can for themselves and not rely upon you to do it! Give your associates the responsibility and authority to solve their own problems and

119

then hold them accountable to do so—whether the problems are "personal" (such as finding out how many vacation days they have left), with coworkers (such as squabbles over work space or methods), or work problems (such as achieving the work group's metrics).

The Personal Action Register is a leadership GPS system tool—part of the accountability system—that empowers team members and reduces your need to be involved in problems they can solve for themselves. And, it fiercely reinforces the fragile, nonnegotiable and negotiable behavioral norms you and your team established in Chapter 5.

The way it works is simple: When an associate asks the supervisor to do something, the supervisor coaches the individual how to do it himself, completes a copy of the Personal Action Register, and gives a copy to the associate, while retaining one for herself.

The supervisor consults her copy of the Personal Action Register and follows up with the associate to find out the outcome. If further action is required, it is noted. If the action is completed, it is also noted. If the team member did not take action—shirked his accountability—the supervisor also takes note and addresses the situation with the individual.

How to use the Personal Action Register

1. **Write down the required action.** Under the Action column, briefly describe what the team member needs to do to correct the problem, such as "See Bob in HR to find out about OT pay."

2. **Note the person responsible.** The "R" column is who will be responsible. Usually this is the team member. Sometimes it might be you, if the action is out of the scope of the individual to accomplish.

3. **Write down the target date.** By when will the task be done?

4. **Note the completion date.** When you follow up with the team member, note the date the task was completed. (If it was not completed, the individual may need more coaching.)

The Personal Action Register is a great tool to use to coach team members on how to solve problems, and it is a great tool for following up—often, unfortunately, a supervisory weakness. And, through its design, it not only empowers but it engages.

In our experience, businesses that opt to use the Personal Action Register find that, after about nine months of consistent use, the dependency cycle is broken; the new norms are well established: Associates take it upon themselves to solve problems they formerly relied on their supervisors to do.

How conceptual accountability transformed into real accountability

A large cosmetics manufacturer struggled with conceptual versus real accountability. Associates were exposed to countless seminars on empowerment and accountability, so conceptually they knew what was expected of them. However, the basic interactions between leaders and associates still demonstrated a relationship of dependency. In other words, team members did not "do" for themselves — they relied on their supervisors to act on their behalf and solve their problems, both big and little.

Leaders decided to tackle the problem by using the Personal Action Register. When all of the leaders began carrying a pad of Personal Action Registers in their lab coat pocket, and to use them consistently, a remarkable transformation began to occur: Team members began to learn a lesson in discernment:

What the leaders observed was that as team members accepted accountability for their own issues, they quickly began to discern between issues that were truly pertinent and meaningful and those that were mere complaints. Supervisors found themselves with more time because associates either realized that their complaint or request was trivial (and subsequently dropped it) or they took it upon themselves to solve their problems.

Leaders often tell their associates, "Don't bring me a problem if you are not willing to be part of the solution." When the organization does not provide a process to move from venting or complaining to fixing or improving, the "problem-solution" admonishment falls on deaf ears. The Personal Action Register, however, gives leaders the ability to listen to issues and then effectively transfer the responsibility of fixing that issue to the appropriate individual.

The Personal Action Register allows for the migration from dependency to interdependency within the leader/associate relationship.

CHAPTER 10

Continuing Your "Trip" through Productive Meetings

G abby gives us coordinates for our destination, but she doesn't drive the car. We do. As we adopt goals, the Business Scorecard, and the other elements of the leadership GPS process, we still have to rely on our "drivers"—our team members— to get the work done. We need them engaged.

We began the engagement process when we set our interpersonal and leadership skills parameters (Chapters 4, 5, 6, and 7). We built on it by applying our accountability system (Chapters 8 and 9). Now we can improve associate engagement by applying leadership GPS's communication system.

It is no surprise to us that when we go into an organization and do a communication assessment we hear these complaints from team members:

- "By the time I hear about something, it is too late. We'll get information on a problem that happened weeks before. We can't do anything about it then."

- "I only hear from my boss when there is a problem."
- "Communication? That's a joke. The grapevine is more reliable than our newsletter."
- "My boss is a terrible communicator. People in other departments always know what's happening long before we get the news."
- "I get tons of e-mail each day. Most I don't even open. It's too hard to keep up."
- "When we get information—and that's not often—it comes down to us. 'They' never listen to us, even though we have good ideas."

These criticisms are indicative of broken communication. Despite the defensive posture of the company's executives who claim they have excellent communication with their team members, we find that their efforts are almost always what we call "advertising." These companies rely on old standbys such as the following:

- A company intranet, on which information about policies, procedures, and company news is posted
- Check stuffers, which may announce changes in policies or reminders of upcoming events
- Bulletin boards, which carry mandatory postings as well as company notices and quality or production numbers
- Newsletters, often mailed to the home
- Meeting minutes, inconsistent in content (depending upon who writes them) and usually sent by e-mail
- E-mailed memos and reports

Figure 10-1 E-Mails, Bulletin Boards

All of these information-sharing devices fail at *true* communication, which is defined as the face-to-face giving and receiving of information, with the opportunity to respond— a two-way exchange. Each traditional communication vehicle admittedly does a fine job of broadcasting information, but the information only flows one way. The sender never knows if the recipient got the information, let alone read it or understood it. It's too easy for someone to walk by the bulletin board without looking at it, to toss the pay envelope in the trash after pulling out the paycheck stub, to throw the newsletter into the pile of junk mail, and to delete e-mails unopened.

The solution to this problem of broken communication is to implement a *communication system* that consistently replicates itself throughout the organization to assure a two-way information flow with active face-to-face engagement between senders and receivers.

Surprised that a weekly meeting could actually help you *do* business? Meetings can—and should—be enablers of the business, not something considered "in addition to" the business. Perhaps you are like the executive we met at a large aerospace company. While we were taking a tour of the facility, a senior VP approached us with a piece of paper in his hand. He wanted to make a point regarding his weekly schedule. Handing us the copy of his weekly Outlook calendar, he said, "Look at all these meetings! I am booked all day, every day. How am I supposed to get any work done?"

He was obviously frustrated, because he (and the organization) considered meetings something *in addition to* the work that had to be done. The meetings the executive was scheduled to attend obviously were failing to do what they *should* have been doing—moving the business forward.

What does it take to have a meeting that moves the business forward? Simply put, the meeting must be *about business*. And the best way to make sure the meeting is about business is to focus the meeting on the Business Scorecard.

To accomplish a business-driven meeting, the team must have a scorecard that sets the tone for the meeting so personalities don't have to. The team should be able to walk into the meeting and within five seconds know the tone and duration of the meeting—"Did we win or lose?" by looking at the scorecard and its visual tracking—green and red.

In essence, the scorecard facilitates the meeting. In the absence of the scorecard facilitating the meeting, the concept of winning and losing is lost and the meeting will degenerate to

be devoted to this item. The team discusses anything in the red—and makes an Action Register to correct problems or to make improvements.

3. **Around the table.** Every team member gets the opportunity to share concerns, problems, and accomplishments and bring up questions. If an issue comes up, the team discusses it. If the issue cannot be answered or addressed immediately, it goes on the Action Register with a target date for completion and someone responsible for solving it. Going around the table is a way to enhance team-member engagement.

4. **Recognition.** Recognition—a pat on the back—is an agenda item. Admittedly, there may not be any recognition to be given every week. But by putting the item on the agenda, it is a trigger for anyone—team leader or team member—to pat someone on the back for a job well done or for going the extra mile. Any recognition made should be put on the "pass up/pass down" list.

5. **Pass up/pass down.** This is a crucial conduit for the briefings of key business information that everyone in the organization needs to know. When a team has a question that needs to be answered from "above," it goes on the pass-up list. Likewise, recognitions go on the list. On the pass-down list are items passed down from above. This pass up/pass down agenda item assures that communication is thoroughly disseminated in a face-to-face, timely manner.

6. **Action Register review No. 2.** Before the meeting is adjourned, the team reviews the Action Register

again—going over any new items added to the Action Register during the meeting to make sure there is a clear understanding about assignments and agreed-upon target dates. Each person who is named on the Action Register should affirm verbally that he or she knows what to do as well as the target date for completion. Review No. 2 is a critical element of the meeting. If it is not done correctly, the next meeting will not start off well.

7. **Meeting audit.** The last item on the standard agenda is "meeting audit." It only takes a few minutes to answer the question, "Did this meeting advance the business?" If members give the meeting a thumbs down, then they must decide what has to be changed to make the meeting better. The goal is to have a productive meeting—not one that just takes more time away from everyone's busy schedule.

When associates are forced to attend unproductive meetings that leave unresolved items, have no agendas, and go on interminably, they complain—around the water cooler, at the copy machine, in each other's offices, around a work station. They talk about how bad the meeting was, how much time was wasted, and how they wished they could get out of going.

The complaints may be legitimate, but they are ill-timed. Complaints—coupled with suggestions on how and what to improve in the meeting—belong *in* the meeting, when the right people are in place to make changes in how the next meeting will be run. And the right time in the meeting to make those complaints and suggestions is during the meeting audit.

Meetings soar to success

A large aerospace manufacturer uses a standard meeting agenda to cascade information down from the top and to get input from all teams. On Monday mornings the senior team meets at 9 a.m. and talks about critical information that needs to be sent down the ranks throughout the organization. One person writes up the information and gives a copy to every team member. Each member of the senior team is a team leader of the next lower-level team. Thus these team leaders take the information and pass it down the line. The process is continued until all teams down the line and across the organization have exactly the same information that was communicated in the top-level meeting.

Using this standard meeting agenda assures consistency and clarity. Because everyone must participate in a weekly team meeting—a nonnegotiable—everyone is guaranteed to have the same information in a timely manner. And because it is transmitted in a face-to-face fashion in a meeting, everyone has the opportunity to make sure they comprehend the information.

A *final note*: Team members, tainted by having attended a multitude of poor meetings over the years, often protest when they find they have to attend yet another meeting each week. "I don't have time!" they declare. What they often find, however, is that within a relatively short time after starting the

Business Scorecard meeting process, the need for other meetings goes away! The number of meetings they have to attend is reduced, the time spent in any of the meetings is productive, and they feel connected to the business because their contributions move the business forward.

Business scorecards → Connectivity
Accountability → Consistency
Communication → Clarity

RECALCULATING

Once we have programmed Gabby with our settings and our destination and we are under way, she tells us, "Please follow the highlighted route." All we have to do is follow her directions.

On her monitor we can see the path she has drawn for us in vivid pink. It's a visual alert. As long as we stay on that pink line, we are OK. But as soon as we cross it by missing a turn, Gabby promptly (and annoyingly) lets us know: "Recalculating! Recalculating!" She takes our error into consideration and advises us how to make the fastest correction to get back on course.

Sometimes—albeit rarely—Gabby makes a mistake. When we were on a trip in the Dallas area recently, Gabby kept giving us wrong directions. The reason was obvious: We were traveling on roads that were being reconstructed with additional lanes and new on/off ramps. We had not updated Gabby's maps, so her information was outdated. Even with the newest maps, construction was occurring so rapidly (and making a temporary mess of the road system!) that we would have had to use our own judgment to get back on track.

Lessons for leadership GPS? We think so.

In this section, we'll look at how the leadership GPS process keeps us on track:

CHAPTER 11

When the Scorecard Turns Red (or Too Green)

Gabby can be so annoying! Once she gets it into her "head" where we should be going, if we deviate just a bit—say, to fill the tank up with gas or to get an ice cream cone—she blares out, "Recalculating! Recalculating!" Despite the nagging, however, we're glad that Gabby keeps us on the straight and narrow. We rarely get lost anymore, thanks to her audible and visual guidance.

Leadership GPS also guides us to keep us on the "straight and narrow" of achieving our goals. Although we don't get an audible signal when we're off track, the Business Scorecard "loudly" tells us where we stand. With a quick glance, we know if we are winning (green) or losing (red).

Thanks to our communication system, which causes us to meet and talk about our scorecards each week, we receive timely information on how we are doing. If we are in the red, we need to make a change—and we can do it in time to make a difference. (That's the difference between leadership GPS's scorecard and other scorecards; integration with

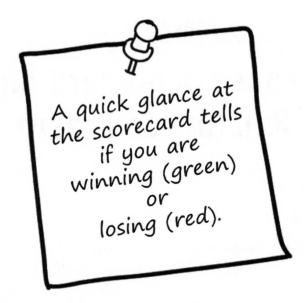

A quick glance at the scorecard tells if you are winning (green) or losing (red).

Figure 11-1 A Quick Glance

the Action Register lets us treat metrics in time to effect real change.) Red tells us that what we are doing is *not enough* or *not correct*.

Of course, there may be reasonable causes for being in the red—such as the supplier didn't ship materials on time, or a blizzard in Minnesota closed down roads for three days straight. Those reasons should be noted in the comments or notes section of the scorecard. And if red is caused because of those reasons, it is possible no action needs to be taken.

But be realistic: Blizzards don't happen every day. And if a supplier is consistently late, perhaps a corrective action (getting a new supplier) is needed.

What is called for when we "see red" on the scorecard is creating a corrective action—a corrective action plan.

5 reasons why you need to use an Action Register

The Action Register is a primary tool to engage team members.

1. It breaks the culture of dependency on the leader.
2. It drives collective engagement with teamwork.
3. It brings visibility to accountability and engagement for both associates and leaders.
4. It eliminates ignorance as an excuse.
5. It raises the bar on expectations.

The Action Register, as we noted in Chapter 9, provides us with an action plan—how we are going to accomplish our metric—for each of the two or three goals that we set under each of the Key Business Focus Aeas (KBFAs) passed down to us from top leadership. The Action Register, however, is also the format in which we make *corrective action plans*—plans to "recalculate" our metrics. Whenever a metric is in the red, we need to develop a corrective action plan and record it in the Action Register.

Sometimes these corrective action plans are very simple.

For example: One of a team's goals is "to maintain production uptime at 98% throughout the fiscal year." A weekly report is required. In the weekly meeting, the owner of the goal reports that uptime has dropped to 95%. In the comments, he writes, "Repair parts did not come in."

The team completes a corrective action: "Find out by Tuesday p.m. when repair parts can be expected." The action item is assigned to Peter.

At other times, however, a corrective action may require more than a simple telephone call. It may require a problem-solving meeting to resolve an involved issue that requires research, testing, funding, purchasing equipment, or other matters.

The weekly Business Scorecard meeting is *not* the place to conduct such a meeting. Rather, it should be done in a separate, dedicated and structured problem-solving meeting. However, the Action Register *should* make note of the action as follows:

Conduct problem-solving meeting to find cause of increased scrap production. Meeting to be conducted by Thursday. Responsible party: Mary.

Mary would be responsible for gathering the proper meeting participants, conducting the meeting, and updating the Action Register by the next weekly meeting.

Leave it to the team

A consumer products company we work with in Kansas City has a rule worth emulating: When a Business Scorecard metric turns red, it is the team's business to turn it green. No manager is allowed a say in how to change the red to green for 30 days. On Day 31, management can insert itself—but not before.

> The company reports that 85% of the time, the team comes up with a plan and changes red to green within the 30 days. They can do this more easily than anyone else because they are closest to the business.

You might be surprised to know that seeing red is not the only time to create a corrective action plan. Seeing too much *green* also calls for corrective action!

Yes, green is good. But too much green may indicate that the metric is no longer challenging or meaningful. So, if a metric on your team's scorecard has remained green for 90 to 120 days or more, consider adding to your Action Register a plan to strengthen and stretch your goals.

When you use the Action Register to capture corrective action plans for every metric in the red and for those in the green for too long a time, you make the business scorecard a dynamic document. You increase its effectiveness. You'll witness the following:

- **Improved performance.** Because your work group "recalculates" in a timely manner, it pushes the business forward, not stagnating under old information.
- **Collective engagement.** It's nice when you know you can count on a few of your team members to get the department through a rough time. But it's even better when the whole team works together with a dedicated engagement that tells you everyone is on the same business page. The scorecard belongs to everyone, not just the leaders of the organization.

- **Continuous improvement.** As your team embraces the idea that too much green on a scorecard is not necessarily good, it sets new, more challenging goals and moves the business forward beyond what was thought possible. They find that incremental change yields great results.

A six-step problem-solving approach

When the team comes together for a separate meeting to problem solve for an issue, it should be done systematically, in order to consider all probable causes and solutions. This six-step approach is recommended:

1. **Define the problem.** In a sentence, describe what occurs, when and how often it occurs, and under what conditions it occurs.

2. **Describe the objective.** What should solving the problem achieve?

3. **Identify possible causes and narrow the causes down to the "killer" causes.** Killer causes are those most likely to be the source of the problem.

4. **Develop solution(s) that will eliminate the cause(s).**

5. **Evaluate solution(s).** Solutions should be evaluated in terms of cost, ease of application, whether they are within the team's control, and other criteria the team establishes.

6. **Select and implement the solution.**

CHAPTER 12

Improving Performance and Engagement

The Business Scorecard originates at the top of the business and cascades down and throughout the organization. Through this system everyone uses a common business language, and all teams create goals and objectives that tactically support the strategic goals and objectives of the organization. And everyone in the organization reviews the status of their goals every week.

But goals, by their nature, are precarious: Many things outside of our control can influence their achievement—the economy, suppliers, even the weather! (A blizzard, a hurricane, or even heavy rains and flooding can cause the best-planned schedules to go awry.) All of these things can cause goals to go unmet.

Then take the metric itself. Sometimes we get caught up in the enthusiasm and passion of furthering the business and we plan too much. Goals need to make us stretch, but they also need to be attainable. If we can't reach them, no matter how hard we try, our scorecard will be in the red.

Sometimes the goal is right—the organization is aiming at the right target—but the *owners* are incorrect. If the team cannot effect the change needed to achieve the goal, the scorecard will be in the red. Or, perhaps the goal is right, but those responsible for achieving it aren't really working toward their goal.

And sometimes the goal is right, but it does not stretch. Goals that are too easy to achieve do not help further the business, nor are they satisfying to the team.

How can you know exactly what is going on? In a word, *audit*. An audit is a look back to see trends, conditions, and causes. Once you identify these, you can address them appropriately. You can use the audit to revise scorecards, identify and implement best practices, and improve accountability and engagement.

Scorecard Revision

You might think that once you and your team completed the hard work of developing your Business Scorecard's metrics, you were done with that activity until next year.

Wrong!

Business Scorecards evolve over time. What seemed like an important and urgent goal when you completed the first iteration of the process might not fall into the same category weeks or months down the line, and a previously unforeseen challenge might present itself as a challenge to business growth. Flexibility is key.

To recognize those challenges, however, and to make sure your scorecard remains a "living" asset replete with metrics that drive the business, it is necessary to conduct an audit—a scorecard reconciliation—every 90 days in a special audit meeting. The purpose of the meeting is to assess the relevancy of scorecard goals and to modify them, if necessary. In this meeting, you want to do three things:

- Check trends
- Review corrective actions and impact
- Ask questions

Although it is possible to self-audit your scorecard, you will receive more realistic and objective feedback if you engage in a more creative auditing process. Here, for example, are three ways we have seen companies audit their scorecards:

- In one company, the top leadership team randomly divides up the number of subordinate teams and assigns them to the various top leaders. The leader each week selects one of the teams and attends its weekly meeting and provides feedback to the team on how it is doing its business.
- In another company, the executive team invites an entire subordinate team to sit in on its weekly meeting. In this way, the subordinate team—which can be from anywhere in the company—helps hold the executive team accountable to do as it "preaches."
- In a third company, teams invite other peer-level teams to their meetings. Not only do they get feedback on how they are moving the business forward, they also get the opportunity to share best practices.

Scorecard myth

Myth: The scorecard is a "done deal," etched in concrete, once metrics are placed on it.

Reality: It takes about three to six iterations (revisions) or scorecards before a team has a real working tool that drives the business forward.

Check trends

In the meeting, look at the scorecard with objective eyes. What does it tell you? Look for trends that indicate goals in need of adjustment, elimination, or replacement.

Metrics that have remained green for 90 days provide an opportunity to raise the target in order to drive continuous improvement. Or these same goals may no longer be relevant. Perhaps the situation that merited them has been resolved. In that case, new, more relevant goals are needed.

Metrics that have stayed in the red—yet have a valid corrective action plan—also need to be reviewed closely. Perhaps the goals are too far reaching and need to be broken down. Some good problem solving may be needed to find the killer cause of why the metric is still in the red and what the team can do about getting it in the green.

Review corrective actions and impact

As you look at trends, consider if a corrective action will improve results. If your work group is unable to impact the metric with a corrective action plan, perhaps the goal is not relevant to your group and should be eliminated from your scorecard.

Ask questions

The meeting should be conducted with an open mind for challenging status quo. Ask the following:

- **Where did the metric come from?** Why did we put it on our scorecard in the first place? If the metric does not provide meaningful data, it should be revised, replaced, or removed.
- **Does the metric tell us if we are winning or losing?** Everything on the scorecard should be driving the business and tied to the business's strategy and priorities.
- **Does the metric truly "belong" to the team—that is, is achieving it within your work group's realm?** If not, it shouldn't be on your scorecard; perhaps it is better suited for another team.
- **Does the team have too many metrics to monitor and work effectively?** If you have too many, the team can lose its sense of priorities and business focus.

Best Practices

A regular audit of scorecards should give rise to something that can improve the overall business: identification of best practices.

Best practices, as you know, are ways of doing something that get consistently superior results, compared to other ways of doing something for the same end. Best practices are important, because they can save time and money by standardizing methodologies and equipment. Consistency—one of leadership GPS's tenets—is a key leadership process.

We recommend a monthly meeting or conference call (or web meeting) to compare performance across plants, sites, or locations, using the Business Scorecards as the "talking stick." Because all teams use the same scorecard format, all goals are based on the same KBFAs, and everyone "talks" the same language, this type of comparison is easily done.

When you meet:

- **Look for best practices.** Teams that consistently achieve their metrics and/or quickly dig themselves out of the red may have something positive to share with teams that are having trouble.
- **Consider local issues versus global issues.** Not every problem applies; look for similarities, not dissimilarities, when you discuss issues.
- **Share corrective actions of things that worked and didn't work.** Sometimes sharing what went wrong (and why) is just as insightful as sharing what went right (and why).

Accountability Analysis

We've said over and again how important employee engagement is to the organization. Those organizations that demonstrate

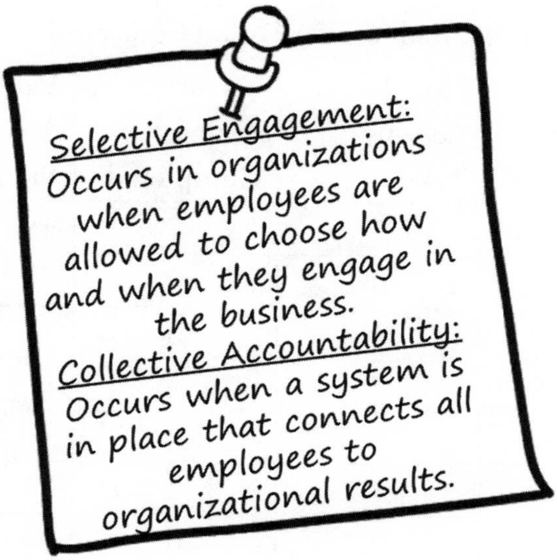

Selective Engagement:
Occurs in organizations
when employees are
allowed to choose how
and when they engage in
the business.
Collective Accountability:
Occurs when a system is
in place that connects all
employees to
organizational results.

Figure 12-1 Selective Engagement

high levels of collective team-member engagement (compared to *selective engagement,* in which only a few are engaged) consistently achieve high levels of success.

How can you tell if your team members are truly engaged? Fortunately the leadership GPS process gives us a method—through an analysis of the Action Register. This is called an accountability analysis. This review accomplishes the following:

- Identifies who is engaged and who is not
- Provides you with data to use in performance reviews as well as to drive recognition to those who deserve it
- Gives you feedback concerning your leadership

Accountability Analysis: For Period from April 1 to June 1			
Name	No. of Actions Taken	No. of Actions Completed	Value of Actions to the Business
Tom	7	7	3.0
Mary	0	0	0
Debra	2	0	0
Adam	4	4	1.0
Patricia	0	0	0
Sherry	5	3	3.0
Larry	0	0	0
Connie	8	3	2.8

Value key: 1 = low; 2 = medium; 3 = high

Five steps are involved in doing an accountability analysis:

1. Draw a chart.
2. Enter the data.
3. Assess the value of actions.
4. Analyze the results.
5. Share the results.

Draw a chart

The chart should have four columns, labeled "name," "actions taken," "actions completed," and "value of actions to the business."

Enter the data

Gather data from the Action Register for the last 90 days and populate the first three columns accordingly. You do this by merely totaling the number of times each of the team members was responsible for an action.

Assess the value of the actions

For each action of each team member, assign a value: 1 = low value to the business; 2 = medium value; and 3 = high value. Average all the values and enter the number in the appropriate column. Although the value is a more subjective assessment, it is also a very telling number, indicating if some individuals are only engaged in low-value actions.

Analyze the results

The results should be apparent: Who is highly engaged? Who is not? Where should you spend more of your time coaching? Are you depending on some people too often, especially in high-value assignments? To get more people engaged, you are highly engaged *not* to volunteer for s involved (such as

e the results with the ɔw who is involved.

Discuss with the team, "What does this analysis tell us? How can we improve?"

Finally, repeat this analysis every 90 days. It will provide you with current data to improve team performance as well as individual performance. The analysis will show you the level of engagement each of your team members has—the high performers and those who are not as actively engaged. It will show if the leader is managing by process or by personality. (If by personality, engagement will be selective, since the leader will rely on the "go to" people. If by process, however, engagement will be collective, with all team members actively participating in moving the business forward.)

ARRIVING!

Gabby is quite a "girl." She guides us effortlessly through traffic, recalculates when we stray from her directions, and then finally tells us when we get to our destination. It is probably our imagination, but we envision her smiling broadly when she announces, "arriving at your destination." She knows she did "good."

We don't have to pat Gabby on the back for a job well done (although sometimes we might feel like it, especially if the trip has been especially challenging), but we do need to recognize our associates for their contributions.

Chapter 13: Celebrate!

Chapter 14: Sustaining Success

CHAPTER 13

Celebrate!

Some trips that we take in our car are pretty straightforward. Getting from point A to point B, with or without Gabby's help, is no big deal. Others, however, are a different story.

We recall one trip in particular. Our destination was in a business complex outside of Dallas, Texas. We kept one eye on Gabby's outlined route (a pink line), and another on the road as we listened to Gabby tell us to turn, then turn again.

We missed our turn. "Recalculating," she chanted. It seemed as though every correction we made did not satisfy her, and she'd come back with her annoying taunt. Eventually, however, we found the right route amid the never-ending Texas highway construction. And we finally reached our destination. We felt like celebrating when Gabby said, "Arriving at your destination on the left."

That's how your team feels—individually and collectively—when they accomplish something tough, or they've gone the "extra mile." They feel like celebrating—and rightfully so.

Celebrating success is essential, but we must do so responsibly—always relating success to the reality of the business. Failing to do so could backfire and result in a sense of entitlement.

Consider what we observed at a family-owned commercial goods manufacturer a few years ago, during the height of the Great Recession.

It had been a tough year, with the recession taking an early toll on the company. A number of people had been laid off; many associates were doing the work of two; everyone was working hard. Because of the sacrifices everyone had made, however, the company had managed to survive.

The owner of the company wanted to reward and recognize his employees with what he thought was a generous a Christmas gift. Aside from the usual Christmas turkey, he had never given a holiday gift to his associates before.

All of the employees gathered at the annual holiday luncheon. When the dining was done, the owner announced to his employees, "Everyone knows we've gone through some tough times. We've seen business slack off, and we had to lay off some good people. The rest of you picked up the slack, and we came through the worst of it OK. I want to thank you for a job well done. To recognize your efforts, I have a surprise for you. As you leave here, go to the loading dock where you will find a truck from Best Buy. There you can pick up a gift from the company—a flat screen HDTV."

The announcement was met with cheers and applause.

The gratitude, however, was short-lived. The gift-giving did not go as planned.

In the weeks before the luncheon, rumors that the company had achieved a profitable year had spread throughout the company. However, no one knew exactly what "profitable" meant. Were the profits $1 million, $10 million, or perhaps even $100 million? All anyone knew was that the owner of the company, who served as company president, was driving a new European sports sedan. The expensive car was their metric for success.

So, when they lined up to get their television, most employees felt they were entitled to a significant reward. They expected at least a 40-inch TV for all their hard work. Imagine their dismay and (vocal) disappointment when each was handed a 13-inch television.

The good intentions of the president backfired. Instead of walking away from the luncheon with a smile on their faces, the associates went back to work feeling scornful and mumbling about the cheapskate in the front office.

Why did this happen? In the absence of a robust and cohesive business process, ignorance and entitlement inevitably prevail. Associates believe "I deserve" instead of "I appreciate." Our data suggest that if associates do not have a robust knowledge and understanding of the business, a culture of entitlement may develop and endure.

If associates within the organization do not understand the business, their knowledge is predicated on what they *do* understand—how hard they are working. If associates don't understand the fundamentals of the business and what defines success, their frame of reference rests solely on their belief that they have worked very hard and deserve more than they have received.

What does all this mean to you? Celebrate success! It's a good thing to do. But celebrate responsibly by correlating the success to the reality of the business through weekly Business Scorecard meetings. Your team will know if the business is winning or losing—and by how much. And they (and you) can plan your celebration accordingly.

When employees accomplish something tough or they have gone the "extra mile," they will like celebrating. Encourage them and join in! It is essential.

Figure 13-1 When Employee Accomplish

Often the best celebration for a job well done doesn't cost a penny. It is recognition from those who count—people like you and your boss. Leadership GPS has a recognition process built into its communication system. It's just up to you to make sure you take advantage of it.

An inappropriate goal

In a company in which we did a communications audit, we discovered that team members felt their extra efforts were going unnoticed. Their usual complaint was, "They are quick to tell you when you are doing a rotten job. But we never hear when we are doing good."

In an effort to correct that situation, the top leaders mandated that every manager and supervisor have a goal of patting someone on the back four times a month (once a week). At the end of the month, it was not unusual to see managers out on the floor, randomly shaking someone's hand and saying, "Thanks for a job well done." They all wanted to make their monthly goal.

The company soon learned that it could not set a measurable goal of giving praise. Instead of being valued by team members, the thanks they gave was received with a cold shoulder.

You will recall that one item on our weekly scorecard meeting is "recognition." We don't recommend setting goals to give a certain amount or type of recognition. Instead, we recommend putting recognition on the agenda of the weekly meeting. It serves as a trigger: You or any other member of the work group can (and should) give a pat on the back to anyone who deserves it that week. Public acknowledgment of a job well done goes a long way. And if no one deserves to be recognized that week? No harm, no foul. Go on to the next agenda item.

Whenever recognition is given in the meeting, it should be noted on the "pass up" notes. Leaders at each progressively higher level of the organization should then take it upon themselves to acknowledge the recognition with their own compliments. If possible, this should be a quick visit to the individual meriting the pat on the back. A personal thank you and a handshake cost nothing but are invaluable. If a personal visit cannot be done in a timely

A handshake, pat on the back, and a simple "thank you" are the least expensive forms of recognition that deliver the most valuable ROI.

Figure 13-2 A Handshake

manner, then an e-mail or a personal handwritten note (much better than an impersonal e-mail) from the leader can substitute.

Giving a pat on the back costs nothing, but when it is given in a sincere manner and is specific concerning why it is deserved, it makes a person feel special. That glow lights up the workplace, and everyone benefits from it.

How to give a pat on the back

Giving informal recognition to someone who deserves it is similar to giving feedback. The main difference is that when you give feedback (correction), you do it in private. When you give a pat on the back, you do it in public. And when you do it, use the SBI method—give the situation, the behavior, and the impact.

Don't wait for an "ideal" time to say thank you. Do it in a timely manner (within 48 hours of the event), and then do it again in your weekly meeting. Here are four steps to simple but effective recognition:

- Publicly thank the individual for a job well done.
- Describe what the person did to deserve the recognition. Tell why it was important.
- Explain how the action affects the organization.
- Pass the recognition up to your boss.

CHAPTER 14

Sustaining Success

Well, there you have it: Our leadership GPS process.

When you use your car's GPS system appropriately—putting in the correct settings and destination, following its guidance, and celebrating when you successfully arrive at your intended geographic target—you get a gratifying feeling that you arrived safe and sound, without getting lost.

We recall that when we first started using Gabby, the process seemed a bit strange. After all, we'd been navigating the highways and byways of this country for years without serious mishap. Given a map (and later, MapQuest), we always got to where we wanted to go. And when we occasionally did get lost, it did not mean we were trapped in some type of Twilight Zone; we always got to our destination even if it meant hours of driving in circles, gallons of gas wasted, and a frustration that seriously tempted us to turn around and go home.

When we purchased our GPS system, we had to take time to read the owner's manual, tinker with the virtual buttons, and learn about all the various settings. Then we had to get into the habit of actually using the contraption whenever we got in the car and got ready to take off on a trip. However, with a bit of practice, it did not take long for us to adapt to Gabby. We quickly fell in love with her. She made traveling so much easier and less frustrating than messing with maps.

Sure, we still get turned around occasionally. But we get back on track quickly and easily, and we arrive at our destination emotionally relaxed.

The leadership GPS process works in the same way.

At first, when you start using it, it will feel uncomfortable. But don't shortcut any of the five steps (the sections in this book):

- Acquiring
- Settings
- Where to?
- Recalculating
- Arriving!

Acquiring

You cannot get to where you want to go unless you know your starting place. That's what acquiring is all about—figuring out the status of your goal-setting process, the engagement level of your people, and the condition of the systems that perpetuate business success.

Settings

Just as we determine if we want to avoid tollways or drive the fastest route when using Gabby, you must input your leadership GPS settings. These settings—interpersonal relations, behavioral expectations, feedback processes, and leadership traits—are the underpinnings of an environment in which team members not only thrive but also become engaged in the business of doing business.

Where To?

When we program Gabby, we put in the state, city, and address of our destination. When you program leadership GPS, you put in your goals, based on Key Business Focus Areas (KBFAs) that are universal to your organization. And you enter these goals into one of your business systems, the Business Scorecard, which serves as a template for all teams within your organization. You also recognize that the drivers of the Business Scorecard are your team members. So you take extra effort to use leadership GPS's accountability and communication systems to engage them to a level of sustaining success. The weekly scorecard meeting is invaluable in doing this.

Recalculating

Sometimes we get off course when we are driving to our destination. Gabby "recalculates" until we get back on track. The

Action Register keeps you on target and helps you to recalculate to improve your business outcomes.

Arriving!

Getting to our destination is sometimes a cause for celebration, especially if our trip has been hazardous or mentally taxing. And so it is, too, when you accomplish the metrics you entered on your Business Scorecard. You should celebrate as a team, and you should always celebrate milestones with appropriate recognition of team members.

That's it—leadership GPS in a nutshell. As we said, when you start this process, you may feel uncomfortable. But within a short time, you will wonder how you ever managed your business without it.

Our thanks to Gabby: May she never lead us astray!

APPENDIX I
Cultural Differences

When individuals from different cultures come together in the workplace, conflict may occur—not just because of language differences but because of cultural differences, especially when associates are recent immigrants.

Learning about the cultures you supervise is helpful in minimizing conflict and improving communication. Books such as *Kiss, Bow or Shake Hands* (available in several different editions) and *Cultural Intelligence: A Guide to Working with People from Other Cultures* (Brooks Peterson, Nicholas Brealey Publishing, January 2004) are excellent resources.

Here is a brief table, sourced from *Kiss, Bow, or Shake Hands*, that highlights just a few cultural differences among three nationalities: Mexican, Japanese, and Indian.

Cultural Differences among Citizens of Four Countries*				
Country	United States	Mexico	Japan	India
Time	Punctuality is expected.	The Mexican culture does not place high value on punctuality.	Punctuality is valued.	Indians appreciate punctuality but do not always practice it. They do not fully comprehend the Western notion of "time is money."
Gestures	The standard conversational distance is about two feet. Pointing is done with the index finger, although pointing at people is impolite. OK sign is indicated with a circle of the thumb and index finger or with a thumbs up.	To get one's attention, they often use a loud "psst." This is not considered rude. Conversations include a lot of physical contact.	Shrugs and winks mean nothing to native Japanese. OK sign means money. Pointing is impolite. Beckoning "come here" is done with palm down.	To beckon someone, Indians hold the hand out, palm downward, and make a scooping motion with the fingers. Pointing with the finger is considered rude; Indians point with the chin. Winking may be considered an insult or a sexual proposition.

Eye contact	Direct eye contact shows interest and sincerity.	Continued, intense eye contact is considered aggressive and threatening.	Prolonged eye contact is not the norm.	Indians use minimal eye contact. Sustained eye contact, especially between men and women, is not the norm.
Communication styles	Often informal. First names are usually used, even among strangers.	Titles are important to native speakers. Conversations often take place in a closer physical distance than Americans are used to.	The Japanese are comfortable with silence. Work is considered "serious." Conversations take place with people farther apart than Americans are used to.	Titles are important. Indians communicate indirectly and may say what they believe is expected. Their actions, however, speak "louder than words."
Touching	Men and women both shake hands; handshakes are firm. Embracing is usually only done among good friends and family.	Touching: Physical contact is normal during conversations, including touching shoulders or holding an arm.	The Japanese almost never touch at work.	Personal conversation space is 3 or 3 ½ feet apart. Indians generally do not touch when communicating, and men and men and women do not touch.

*Adapted from *Kiss, Bow, or Shake Hands* by Terri Morrison and Wayne A. Conaway, Adams Media (July 2006)

Name of Metric	Frequency of Metric	Key Focus Area/Indicator	Applicable Team	Metric Definition
Number of control improvement initiatives meetings	Monthly/Quarterly	Operational excellence	Operational/Leadership	Improve the number of control improvement initiatives within month/quarter by 10%
Percentage of cross-trained personnel	Monthly/Quarterly	People	Training	Maintain a skilled and experienced workforce
Average production cost per item	Monthly/Weekly	Cost	Production	Average production cost broken out by item
Deviation of planned budget	Weekly/Monthly	Cost	Finance/Leadership	Difference in costs between the planned against the actual budget
Deviation of planned time schedule for project/program	Monthly/Quarterly	Projects/Programs	Operational/Leadership	Difference in time between the planned against the actual schedule
Average number of training hours per employee	Monthly/Quarterly	Training/People	Training/Leadership	Total number training hours divided by the number of employees
Total overtime cost	Weekly/Monthly/Quarterly	Cost/People	Finance/Leadership	Payments paid to employee for work done outside their normal working hours

APPENDIX II
Process-Based Leadership Business Scorecards

The following table lists a number of different types of metrics teams typically use on their business scorecards.

Name of Metric	Frequency of Metric	Key Focus Area/ Indicator	Applicable Team	Metric Definition
Average time from customer request to sales team response	Weekly	Customer satisfaction/ People	Sales/ Marketing	Average time from sales team to customer
Key customer satisfaction	Monthly	Customer satisfaction	Sales/ Marketing	Percentage of key customers that are satisfied with their service
In-house customer satisfaction	Quarterly	Customer satisfaction	All teams	Maintain and improve employee satisfaction by 10% per customer
Customer service requests open over 75 (× days)	Monthly	Customer satisfaction	Operational/ Service	Retention of customers/ minimizing negative comment in the marketplace
Cost of equipment repair	Monthly/ Quarterly	Customer satisfaction/ Cost	Quality/ Finance	Total $ amount of equipment for repair or break downs

(Continued)

171

Name of Metric	Frequency of Metric	Key Focus Area/ Indicator	Applicable Team	Metric Definition
Cost of rework	Weekly	Customer satisfaction/ Quality	Quality/ Operational excellence	Total $ amount of rework per week
Number of stock outs	Weekly	Customer satisfaction/ Quality	Production	Efficiency of operations

Name of Metric	Frequency of Metric	Key Focus Area/ Indicator	Applicable Team	Metric Definition
Customer service cost ratio	Monthly	Customer satisfaction/ People	Sales/ Marketing	Total cost of customer service by the number of customers provided service
Invoice management cost	Monthly/ Quarterly	Customer satisfaction	Sales/ Marketing	Costs for invoicing, processing customer payments, and verifying customer satisfaction
Customer satisfaction with new products/ services	Quarterly	Customer satisfaction	All teams	New products and new services
Customer impact rate	Weekly	Customer satisfaction	Operational/ Service	Number of problems that impacted the customer/ total number of problems during the review period*
Number of problems that impacted the customer	Weekly	Customer satisfaction	Operational/ Service	Number of problems that impacted the customer
Total number of problems during the review period	Weekly	Customer satisfaction	Operational/ Service	Total number of problems during the review period
Engagement to effectiveness	Monthly/ Quarterly	Customer satisfaction	Operational excellence	Number of engagements in area vs productivity gains before and after
Quality of services delivered	Monthly/ Weekly	Customer satisfaction/ Quality	Quality/ Operational excellence	Improve reporting and customer reviews by 20 %

172

Name of Metric	Frequency of Metric	Key Focus Area/ Indicator	Applicable Team	Metric Definition
Number of the new change requests	Weekly	Customer satisfaction/ People	Sales/ Marketing	Measures on change requests that give indication of quality and quantity
Average serving time	Weekly/ Monthly	Customer satisfaction/ Quality	Operational/ Service	Average time that a customer takes seat by the time to being served
% of defect from customer claims	Monthly	Customer satisfaction/ Quality	All teams	The number of goods that have been returned by the number of goods from the customer
Customer injury rate per million	Monthly	Safety/ People	Safety	Rate per million for injuries of customer
Resolution time of complaints	Monthly	Customer satisfaction	Quality	Time from complaint to customer resolution
Number of Incidents logged with no solution	Weekly/ Monthly	Quality/ Customer satisfaction	Quality/ Operational excellence	Number of incidents that were not solved without a solution
Number of customers per server	Monthly	Information technology	Information technology	Number of customers per server per month

Name of Metric	Frequency of Metric	Key Focus Area/ Indicator	Applicable Team	Metric Definition
Accounts receivable turnover	Monthly	Finance/ Cost	Accounting	Number of times accounts receivable are paid and reestablished during period
Bad debt percentage to turnover	Monthly	Finance/ Cost	Accounting	Percentage of bad debt to turnover
Cash flow $	Monthly	Finance/ Cost	Accounting	Total dollar amount of cash flow per month
Contribution margin %	Monthly	Finance/ Cost	Accounting	Percentage of contribution margin
Average days in Accounts Payable	Quarterly	Finance/ Cost	Accounting	Average number of days accounts are payable to creditors

(Continued)

173

Name of Metric	Frequency of Metric	Key Focus Area/ Indicator	Applicable Team	Metric Definition
Net income	Monthly	Finance/ Cost	Accounting	Total net income for month
Profits/ employee	Monthly	Finance/ Cost	Accounting	Total gross operations profits per employee earned
Long-term assets	Monthly	Finance/ Cost	Accounting	Capital assets held for longer than one accounting period
Depletion	Monthly	Finance/ Cost	Accounting	Amortization of assets that can be physically reduced
% Accuracy of periodic financial reports	Quarterly	Finance/ Cost	Accounting	Percentage accuracy of periodic financial reports over a QTR
Accounting costs	Quarterly/ Annual	Finance/ Cost	Accounting	Total accounting expenses within the "X"

Name of Metric	Frequency of Metric	Key Focus Area/ Indicator	Applicable Team	Metric Definition
Average sum deposited in new deposit accounts	Monthly	Finance/Cost/ Account	Finance/ Banking	Average amount deposited in new accounts per month
% of overdue claims	Quarterly	Finance/Cost/ Account	Finance/ Banking	Percentage of overdue claims per month
% of fraudulent insurance claims	Monthly/ Quarterly	Finance/Cos/ Account	Finance/ Banking	Percentage of fraudulent insurance claims
% of fraudulent insurance claims investigated and closed	Monthly/ Quarterly	Finance/Cost/ Account	Finance/ Banking	Percentage of fraudulent insurance claims investigated and closed
Average number of withdraws per ATM location	Weekly/ Monthly	Finance/Cost/ Account	Finance/ Banking	Average number of withdraws per ATM location
% of operating revenue from banking fees	Monthly	Finance/Cost/ Account	Finance/ Banking	Percentage of operating revenue from banking fees
% of overdue premium	Weekly	Finance/Cost/ Account	Finance/ Banking	Percentage of overdue premiums

174

Name of Metric	Frequency of Metric	Key Focus Area/ Indicator	Applicable Team	Metric Definition
% of correspondence replied to on time	Weekly/ Monthly	Quality	Government	Percentage of correspondence replied to on time from date sent
% of households living in the correct townships/ areas	Monthly	People	Government	Percentage of households living in the correct townships/areas that are on record
Number of vehicles accessing the city center	Monthly	Quality	Government	Number of vehicles accessing the city center
Number of older people helped to live at home per 1,000	Monthly	People	Government	Number of older people with assistance to live at home (aged 65 and above)
% of vehicles removed within 24 hours by area	Weekly/ Monthly	Quality	Government	% of vehicles removed within 24 hours by area
% of taxes received by date due	Monthly	Cost/ Finance	Government	Percentage of taxes received by date due
# of expired license plates by county	Monthly	Quality	Government	Number of expired license plates by county

Name of Metric	Frequency of Metric	Key Focus Area/Indicator	Applicable Team	Metric Definition
% of HR budget spent on training	Weekly	Cost/Finance	Human resources	Percentage of human resources spent on Training
HR department cost per FTE	Monthly	Cost/Finance	Human resources	Human resources department cost per full-time employee
Number of positions open	Weekly	People	Human resources	Number of positions open
Number of days a requisition/job has been open	Weekly	People	Human resources	Number of days a requisition/job has been open
On-campus activities per week	Weekly	Operational	Human resources	Number of on-campus activities per week

(Continued)

175

Name of Metric	Frequency of Metric	Key Focus Area/Indicator	Applicable Team	Metric Definition
Number of background checks pending	Weekly	People	Human resources	Number of background checks pending
Number of drug tests pending	Weekly	People	Human resources	Number of drug tests pending
Number of offers that need processing	Weekly	People	Human resources	Number of offers that need processing
Number of on-boarding classes	Weekly	People	Human resources	Number of on-boarding classes

Name of Metric	Frequency of Metric	Key Focus Area/ Indicator	Applicable Team	Metric Definition
Recruitment rating	Quarterly	People	Human resources	Recruitment rating (survey on all new employees)
Number of recruits from employee referrals	Weekly	People	Human resources	Number of recruits from employee referrals
Number of overseas job openings	Monthly	People	Human resources	Number of overseas job openings
Number of overseas transfer processed	Weekly	People	Human resources	Number of overseas transfer processed
Number of applicants for employment at the company	Monthly	People	Human resources	Number of applicants for employment at the company
Employee satisfaction per survey	Quarterly	People	Human resources	Every employee survey per quarter
Number of employees who have received recognition	Weekly	People	Human resources	Number of employees who have received recognition
% of staff working flexible hours	Weekly	People	Human resources	Percentage of staff working flexible hours
Total staff turnover	Monthly	People	Human resources	Staff turnovers totals by sub metrics

Name of Metric	Frequency of Metric	Key Focus Area/ Indicator	Applicable Team	Metric Definition
Staff turnover— resignations	Monthly	People	Human resources	Staff turnover by resignations
Staff turnover—end of contract	Monthly	People	Human resources	Staff turnover by end of contract
Staff turnover— temporary staff	Monthly	People	Human resources	Staff turnover by temporary staff
Staff turnover— terminations	Monthly	People	Human resources	Staff turnover by terminations

Name of Metric	Frequency of Metric	Key Focus Area/ Indicator	Applicable Team	Metric Definition
Average handling cost per insurance claim	Weekly	Cost/Quality	Insurance/ Quality	Average handling cost per insurance claim
Average handling time of insurance claims	Weekly	Cost/Quality	Insurance/ Quality	Average handling time of insurance claims
Average overdue time of insurance claims	Weekly	Cost/Quality	Insurance/ Quality	Average overdue time of insurance claims
Total number Insurance claims immediately processed	Weekly	Cost/Quality	Insurance/ Quality	Total number Insurance claims immediately processed
Number of insurance claims handled correctly	Weekly	Cost/Quality	Insurance/ Quality	Number of insurance claims handled correctly
Number of insurance claims handled incorrectly	Weekly	Cost/Quality	Insurance/ Quality	Number of insurance claims handled incorrectly
Average number of insurance claims per handler	Weekly	Cost/Quality	Insurance/ Quality	Average number of insurance claims per handler
% of incorrectly assigned insurance claims	Weekly	Cost/Quality	Insurance/ Quality	Percentage of incorrectly assigned insurance claims

Name of Metric	Frequency of Metric	Key Focus Area/Indicator	Applicable Team	Metric Definition
% of escalated insurance claims	Weekly/ Monthly	Cost/Quality	Insurance/ Quality	Percentage of escalated insurance claims
Average closure duration of insurance claims	Weekly	Cost/Quality	Insurance/ Quality	Average closure duration of insurance claims
Closure duration rate of insurance claims	Weekly	Cost/Quality	Insurance/ Quality	Duration of insurance claims closed relative to the claims closed in a given time frame
Backlog of insurance claims	Weekly	Cost/Quality	Insurance/ Quality	Number of open insurance claims older than "X" days
% of insurance claims worked on	Weekly	Cost/Quality	Insurance/ Quality	Percentage of insurance claims that could been worked on actually were
% of reopened insurance claims	Weekly	Cost/Quality	Insurance/ Quality	Percentage of reopened (valid) insurance claims
% of claims paid in 30 days	Weekly	Cost/Quality	Insurance/ Quality	Percentage of claims paid in "X" days of receipt
% of neglected insurance claims	Weekly	Cost/Quality	Insurance/ Quality	Percentage of neglected insurance claims

Name of Metric	Frequency of Metric	Key Focus Area/ Indicator	Applicable Team	Metric Definition
Number of customer per server	Weekly/ Monthly	Customer	Information technology	Number of customers per server
% of trials that convert into customers	Weekly/ Monthly	Customer/ Finance	Information technology	Percentage of trials that convert into customers
Total cost per customer per instance	Weekly/ Monthly	Cost/ Finance	Information technology	Total cost per customer per instance

Name of Metric	Frequency of Metric	Key Focus Area/ Indicator	Applicable Team	Metric Definition
Fixed cost per customer per instance	Weekly/ Monthly	Cost/ Finance	Information technology	Fixed cost per customer per instance
Customer retention rate	Weekly/ Monthly	Customer	Information technology	Retained customers over total customers per period
Recurring revenue	Weekly/ Monthly	Cost/ Finance	Information technology	Sum of the monthly contract values
Available cash	Weekly/ Monthly	Cost/ Finance	Information technology	Cash payments from the customer over period

Name of Metric	Frequency of Metric	Key Focus Area/ Indicator	Applicable Team	Metric Definition
Mission-critical downtime %	Weekly	Availability	Operations/ Operational excellence	Critical equipment downtime from 5% to 2% per week
Improve monthly equipment utilization hours	Monthly	Availability	Operations/ Operational excellence	Meet minimum standard of 7.5 hours per 8 hour shift
Units produced per equipment up-time hours	Quarterly	Production	Operations/ Operational excellence	Increase units produced per equipment up-time hours by 5% per QTR
Direct labor costs per 1000 per QTR	Quarterly	Costs/ Finance	Operations/ Operational excellence	Decrease direct labor costs per 1,000 units by 5% per QTR
On time delivery of units shipped	Monthly	Delivery/ Schedule	Operations/ Operational excellence	Increase on time delivery of units shipped from 90% to 95% by end of FY
Hours spent on product reworks per week	Weekly	Quality	Operations/ Operational excellence	Reduce monthly hours spent on product reworks from 4 hours/week to 3 hours/week
% of resource and materials planning accuracy per month	Monthly	Costs/ Finance	Operations/ Operational excellence	Improve resource and materials planning accuracy from 88% to 90% per month
Cycle time over previous production period	Monthly	Production	Operations/ Operational excellence	Improve cycle time over previous production period by 5%

Name of Metric	Frequency of Metric	Key Focus Area/ Indicator	Applicable Team	Metric Definition
Number of defective units per 1,000	Monthly	Quality	Operations/ Operational excellence	Decrease number of defective units per 1,000 during 12-month warranty period from 30 to 20
In-stock critical equipment parts availability	Weekly	Availability	Operations/ Operational excellence	Improve in-stock critical equipment parts availability from 80% to 90%
Number of rework units per 1,000 due to equipment calibration errors	Monthly	Quality	Operations/ Operational excellence	Reduce number of rework units per 1,000 due to equipment calibration errors from 50 to 40
Variance from planned to budget	Monthly	Cost/ Finance	Operations/ Operational excellence	Reduce dollar amount variance from planned budget from $10,000 to $8,000 per month
Loss due to unplanned scrap material	Monthly	Cost/ Finance	Operations/ Operational excellence	Reduce monthly loss due to unplanned scrap materials from $15,000 to $1,000 per month
Number of customer rejects per 100 units	Monthly	Quality	Operations/ Operational excellence	Decrease number of customer rejects per 1,000 units from 12 to 10 per month
Production variance to schedule	Monthly	Schedule	Operations/ Operational excellence	Reduce production variance to schedule from 5% per shift to 2% per shift

Name of Metric	Frequency of Metric	Key Focus Area/ Indicator	Applicable Team	Metric Definition
Equipment down time due to unplanned maintenance-hours	Monthly	Availability/ Schedule	Operations/ Operational excellence	Decrease equipment down time due to unplanned maintenance from 2.5 hours per period to 2 hours per period
% of hourly down time operational costs	Monthly	Costs/ Finance	Operations/ Operational excellence	Decrease hourly down time operational costs by 20% over same period last year

180

Name of Metric	Frequency of Metric	Key Focus Area/ Indicator	Applicable Team	Metric Definition
Down time due to lack of materials — hours	Monthly	Availability/ Schedule	Operations/ Operational excellence	Decrease down time due to lack of materials (not equipment issues) from 1.5 hours per month to 1 hour per month
Shift change down time — minutes	Weekly	People	Operations/ Operational excellence	Reduce shift change down time from 25 minutes a day to 15 minutes a day
Operations certifications training test scores	Quarterly	People	Operations/ Operational excellence	Improve equipment operations certification training test scores from an average of 87/100 to 95/100 per employee per QTR

Name of Metric	Frequency of Metric	Key Focus Area/ Indicator	Applicable Team	Metric Definition
Equipment availability %	Weekly/ Monthly	Production/ Operations	Production/ Operations	Percentage of equipment available during production
Equipment performance %*	Weekly/ Monthly	Production/ Operations	Production/ Operations	Percentage of equipment performance* (operating time/planned production time)
Operating time	Weekly/ Monthly	Production/ Operations	Production/ Operations	Total operating time per week/month
Planned production time	Weekly/ Monthly	Production/ Operations	Production/ Operations	Planned production time per week/month
Production cycle time	Weekly/ Monthly	Production/ Operations	Production/ Operations	Time in each cycle of production
Outage hours per month	Weekly/ Monthly	Production	Production	Production outage hours — stoppage
Quality problems due to equipment failure	Weekly/ Monthly	Production/ Quality	Production/ Quality	Equipment failure causing quality issues
Excess inventory counts	Weekly/ Monthly	Production	Production	Count of inventory that is considered excessive

Name of Metric	Frequency of Metric	Key Focus Area/ Indicator	Applicable Team	Metric Definition
% of corrective maintenance cost	Weekly	Production	Production/ Maintenance	Percentage of corrective maintenance costs of total maintenance costs within measurement period.
Maintenance cost per unit*	Weekly	Production	Production/ Maintenance	Total maintenance divided by number of produced units per week/month
Total maintenance costs	Weekly	Production	Production/ Maintenance	Sub metric*
Maintenance cost—man hours	Weekly	Production	Production/ Maintenance	Sub metric*
Maintenance cost—parts	Weekly	Production	Production/ Maintenance	Sub metric*
Number of produced units per week/month	Weekly	Production	Production/ Maintenance	Sub metric*
Backlog of maintenance work orders	Weekly	Production	Production/ Maintenance	Maintenance work based on outstanding work orders
% of preventive maintenance time	Monthly	Production	Production/ Maintenance	Percentage of preventive maintenance time spent per month

Name of Metric	Frequency of Metric	Key Focus Area/ Indicator	Applicable Team	Metric Definition
% of construction and demolition waste recycled	Monthly	Environment/ Safety	Public Works	Percentage of construction and demolition waste recycled
% of household waste sent for recycling	Monthly	Environment/ Safety	Public works	Percentage of household waste sent for recycling
% of works completed within timeframe	Weekly/ Monthly	Quality	Public works	Percentage of work completed within week/ month

Name of Metric	Frequency of Metric	Key Focus Area/ Indicator	Applicable Team	Metric Definition
% of key projects open	Weekly	Quality	Public works	Percentage of key projects currently open per week
Average time to repair traffic lights	Weekly	Quality/ Safety	Public works	Average time to repair traffic lights
% of street/road signs repaired within "X" days	Weekly	Quality/ Safety	Public works	Percentage of street/ road signs repaired within "X" days
% of public transport vehicles running on time	Weekly	Quality	Public works	Percentage of public transport vehicles running on time

Name of Metric	Frequency of Metric	Key Focus Area/ Indicator	Applicable Team	Metric Definition
Turnaround time	Weekly/ Monthly	Quality	Shipping	Average time by arrival of product and departure of product
Average arrivals	Weekly/ Monthly	Quality	Shipping	Sub metric (product arrivals)
Average departure	Weekly/ Monthly	Quality	Shipping	Sub metric (product departure)
% of cargo damaged or lost during Shipping	Weekly/ Monthly	Quality/ Operations	Shipping	Percentage of cargo damaged or lost during shipping
Trailer fill %	Weekly/ Monthly	Quality	Shipping	Total trailer fill percentage
% of customized shipping solutions	Weekly/ Monthly	Quality/ Customer	Shipping	Percentage of customized shipping solutions for clients
Indirect shipping costs	Monthly	Cost/ Finance	Shipping	Total indirect shipping costs
Direct shipping costs	Monthly	Cost/ Finance	Shipping	Total direct shipping costs

Name of Metric	Frequency of Metric	Key Focus Area/ Indicator	Applicable Team	Metric Definition
Average subscription length	Monthly	Customer	Telecommunications	Average subscription length in months
Service downtime %	Weekly/ Monthly	Customer/ Quality	Telecommunications	Percentage of the time service is down
% of dropped telephone calls	Weekly/ Monthly	Customer	Telecommunications	Calls ended to technical failure
% of prepaid subscribers	Monthly	Customer	Telecommunications	Percentage of prepaid subscribers
Average fixed costs per telecom tower	Monthly	Costs	Telecommunications	Average fixed costs per telecom tower
Availability	Monthly	Customer/ Quality	Telecommunications	[Time between failure/(time between failure + time between repair)] × 100
Time between failure	Monthly	Customer/ Quality	Telecommunications	Sub metric
Time to repair	Monthly	Customer/ Quality	Telecommunications	Sub metric

Name of Metric	Frequency of Metric	Key Focus Area/ Indicator	Applicable Team	Metric Definition
% of orders delivered with damaged products/items	Weekly	Quality	Transportation/ Supply chain	Percentage of orders delivered with damaged products/items
Transit time	Weekly	Quality	Transportation	Number of days or hours from time shipment leaves to it arrives
On-time delivery	Weekly	Quality	Transportation	Percentage of shipments which are delivered on time upon total number of goods
Freight cost per unit shipped	Weekly/ Monthly	Cost	Transportation	Total freight cost/ number of units shipped per period

Name of Metric	Frequency of Metric	Key Focus Area/ Indicator	Applicable Team	Metric Definition
Total freight costs	Weekly/ Monthly	Cost	Transportation	Sub metric
Number of units shipped	Weekly/ Monthly	Cost	Transportation	Sub metric
Average consignment size	Weekly/ Monthly	Quality	Transportation	Average consignment size by pallet loads

Name of Metric	Frequency of Metric	Key Focus Area/ Indicator	Applicable Team	Metric Definition
% of time a product is available on the shelf	Weekly	Sales/Cost	Wholesale/ Retail	Total time available/ total time store open
Total time product available	Weekly	Sales/Cost	Wholesale/ Retail	Sub metric
Total time store is open	Weekly	Sales/Cost	Wholesale/ Retail	Sub metric
Time from order creation to service delivery	Weekly	Quality	Wholesale/ Retail	Time from order creation to service delivery
Warehouse productivity level	Weekly/ Monthly	Quality	Wholesale/ Retail	Total amount of pickings/total direct hours spent
Amount of pickings	Weekly/ Monthly	Quality	Wholesale/ Retail	Sub metric
Total direct hours spent	Weekly/ Monthly	Quality	Wholesale/ Retail	Sub metric
New products introduced	Monthly/ Quarterly	Sales	Wholesale/ Retail	New products introduced at retail and added to catalogue
Average number of products in product category	Weekly/ Monthly	Sales	Wholesale/ Retail	Average number of products in product category
% of Items with overdue sales date	Weekly/ Monthly	Sales	Wholesale/ Retail	Percentage of items that are overdue to be sold by sales date

APPENDIX III
Case Studies

Leadership GPS, a focused application of Process-Based Leadership®, is a tried-and-proven system of improving organizational effectiveness. On the following pages are seven case studies that describe real organizational challenges, the solutions that Competitive Solutions, Inc. (CSI) helped implement, and the results that were achieved.

Case Study 1: Cultural Change at Army Industrial Base Maintenance Repair and Overhaul Facility (AIBMROF)

Case Study 2: Measurable Results at Large Scale Military Equipment OEM

Case Study 3: Oil and Gas Processor (OGP) Achieves Lasting Returns

Case Study 4: International Ink Manufacturer (IIM) Gets Great Return

Case Study 5: Private Jet Manufacturer (PJM) Reaches New Heights

Case Study 6: World Class Evaporator Manufacturer Delivers Results

Case Study 7: Army Tactical Assault Vehicle Overhaul Repair Facility Improves Operations

CASE STUDY 1

Cultural Change at Army Industrial Base Maintenance Repair and Overhaul Facility (AIBMROF)

Army Industrial Base Maintenance Repair and Overhaul Facility (AIBMROF) is the largest, full-service electronics maintenance facility in the Department of Defense (DoD). The depot's mission is total sustainment, including design, manufacture, repair, and overhaul of hundreds of electronic systems. Its work includes installing and maintaining satellite terminals, radio and radar systems, telephones, electro-optics, night vision and anti-intrusion devices, airborne surveillance equipment, navigational instruments, electronic warfare, and guidance and control systems for tactical missiles. The installations workload has doubled since 2003. AIBMROF has earned five Shingo medallions of excellence since 2006.

The Challenge

AIBMROF's Systems Integration and Support (SIS) directorate wanted to improve its entire leadership proficiency, from first-line supervisors up to and including the senior staff. The aim was to develop a close-knit team that could effect cultural change throughout the workforce.

AIBMROF needed a fully rounded approach to leadership development that focused on all leadership skills operationally, professionally, and personally. The directorate's senior team wanted to ensure that all managers were fully engaged in executing effective leadership that derived its tenets from its corporate philosophy business model. Prior workforce surveys showed concerns in communication, employee empowerment, trust, diversity, expectations, and motivation at all levels of the organization. The directorate was also concerned that each level of leadership was acting one level below its authority level, with the result that lower levels of leadership depended on senior leaders for all decisions and resolutions.

The Solution

AIBMROF decided to implement Process Based Leadership® in all directorates in 1996 to gain a strong competitive advantage by building upon the integrated foundation processes of communication, accountability, scorecards, and expectations. Process Based Leadership® is the basis of AIBMROF's team-based corporate philosophy and is considered a nonnegotiable business process.

CSI designed and implemented a leadership sustainment system. The program provides all leaders at every level a monthly, four-hour custom class, supplemented with three hours of private coaching and shadowing for each student. The leadership curriculum concentrates upon world-class leadership books, specific coaching actions, and class homework. The class modules include the following:

- Managing multigenerational teams
- Coaching for success
- Performance development
- Sustaining business performance
- Providing behavioral feedback

The Results

Business results include measurable improvement in lost-time accidents, percent of work finished to schedule, a reduction in the amount of rework, and a reduction in indirect labor hours. Surveys indicate improvements in trust, employee morale, customer service, leadership confidence, delegation and empowerment, and subordinate and team development. SIS is the largest directorate within AIBMROF.

This leadership GPS process is now moving into other depots and world-class corporate clients of CSI. Anna VerSteeg, CSI principal, summarizes, "AIBMROF had the vision and inspiration to turn to this CSI system. The results have been extremely successful and life changing, from business, leadership, and personal levels. This has been the most rewarding program I have ever developed and participated in both from a personal and business standpoint. We helped mentor changes in lifestyle, time management, delegation, professional communication, and empowerment. We all learned and grew together."

CASE STUDY 2
Measurable Results at Large Scale Military Equipment OEM

A Large Scale Military Equipment OEM (Original Equipment Manufacturer)—MEOEM—fully embraces the Lean/Six Sigma approach in all facets of its business. It has shown significant improvements in its manufacturing environments and work spaces for safety, housekeeping, productivity, and utilization of space. At MEOEM, the challenge was to extend those gains to include efficiency, teamwork, and elimination of waste, and also to improve overall performance in the administrative offices similar to the improvements made on the shop floors.

The Challenge

Although it utilized Lean/Six Sigma quality control, the organization did use nonnegotiable, minimum standard operating processes. CSI conducted a sitewide assessment, which revealed the following:

- Senior leaders used individual leadership styles, which resulted in confusion and an unclear messages to subordinates.
- Meetings often started late, with key individuals missing. This resulted in poor communications.
- Meeting agendas were not standardized, and meetings were not regularly scheduled.
- Meetings, which lacked structure and process, were often canceled when the leader was not able to attend.
- Action logs were being used inconsistently. In many cases decisions were not being captured and communicated, which resulted in critical tasks not being completed.
- Several different scorecard formats were being used, resulting in data that decision makers could not trust.
- Only 24% of employees could explain how metrics were being calculated and how those metrics could be impacted by their work.
- Only 16% of employees said they used scorecard results consistently to develop new processes and improvement opportunities.
- Problems were being addressed without identifying root causes to drive appropriate decisions and corrective actions.
- The organization lacked processes to deliver formal behavioral expectations. Leaders had to deliver feedback and reviews without supporting data.

The Solution

Beginning with the senior leadership team (SLT), CSI delivered several days of Process Based Leadership® training stressing leadership GPS. The SLT focused on developing a formal communication process to be modeled and replicated in all departments at all levels. The communication process calls for the standardization of home-team meetings. Each home team now follows the same agenda, which includes, at a minimum, a review of current actions, a review of scorecards, employee recognition, and a "pass up/pass down process" for distributing critical information.

Additionally, the SLT clearly defined ground rules for when, where, how, and how often meetings needed to be held. A sitewide communication "waterfall" chart was created so that senior leaders know exactly when each team receives key information each week.

To overcome challenges with accountability, each home-team meeting begins and ends with a review of its Action Register, which includes all current and open actions. Each action states what is to be done, by whom, and a specific target date for completion. Team discussion centers on those actions due at the time of the meeting; problem solving takes place outside of the regular team meetings.

With an eye on increased awareness and overall efficiency, MEOEM also installed PBL Scorecard software to automate all of its processes. The software allows the home-team members to track updated, accurate metric scores alongside their assigned corrective actions. Users are also able to view and discuss critical "pass down" communication items from the SLT. All meeting minutes and notes are also recorded for future review.

The Results

One of the managers of the SLT reported, "The use of PBL in all of our meetings has increased the level of employee engagement throughout the organization. All employees are staying informed of the status of all metrics on their team's scorecard, as well as the site's scorecard. Information is now routinely passed down, across, and up the organizational chain. PBL is certainly helping us to change . . . our culture, for the better, and we all know how difficult it is to change the culture of an organization."

A focused meeting agenda and discussion have improved meeting efficiency. A manager reports, "PBL has allowed us to consistently run our meetings at higher levels, thus allowing us to elevate the overall execution and performance as well. PBL promotes synergy in communications and similar expectations across the site."

Approximately 18 months after initial PBL implementation, Competitive Solutions, Inc., was invited to return and conduct another formal assessment of the MEOEM from top to bottom. Survey results show vast improvements across the four major categories of communication, business focus, accountability, and behavior.

The entire site had made significant strides in improving the way the business is being run. The organization now shares a common vocabulary, communicates via standard home-team meetings, uses a common format for team scorecards, and utilizes action registers for accountability.

Utilizing the principles of PBL and the leadership GPS process, the organization has achieved measureable results:

- **Everyone is on the same page.** With the standardization of meeting agendas and the adherence to a defined communication process, there was a 30% average increase in respondents answering "always" on questions confirming communication effectiveness. A question regarding the sharing of best practices produced a 55% increase in "always" responses.
- **Knowing the business results.** Survey results dealing with the use of scorecards and performance showed a 60% increase in "always" answers by employees. Clearly, more employees are now aware of the metrics being used to measure performance against the stated goals.
- **A more engaged workforce.** Now that communication is better and scorecards are consistently used for all teams at all levels, there has been a 79% increase in "always" responses concerning accountability and a commitment to due dates. Employees now have the ability to accept tasks, complete those tasks, and affect metric scores without the need for constant reminders by their leader.

- **New behaviors.** From top to bottom, employees have shown a change in their behaviors and how they perceive the way decisions are being made in running the business. A positive increase of 38% was shown in the follow-up assessment with regard to how employees see their leaders' understanding of the business, how issues get resolved, and how employees on multiple levels interface to produce positive results.

CASE STUDY 3
Oil and Gas Processor (OGP) Achieves Lasting Returns

Located in South Carolina, the OGP facility sits on more than 5,900 acres of forest and wetlands, making it one of the world's largest purified terephthalic acid (PTA) plants.

The Challenge

Following its latest major merger between two major gas producers, the organization faced several daunting challenges. Over the years, the corporation had acquired a number of other energy companies, resulting in a mix of backgrounds and cultures. Top management realized the need to transition from self-directed work teams to an accountability-driven operating system to achieve uniformity and focus.

OGP's South Carolina facility had four rotating production shifts that faced a variety of challenges, such as the following:

- Communicating important, timely business information to all employees at all levels
- Establishing a common organizational culture
- Integrating a corrective-action process into daily operations

In 2008, OGP began a journey to standardize operations and blend the various cultures into one cohesive operating unit. It launched the Operating Management System (OMS) program to align all operations and cultures more tightly. Fortunately, prior to beginning its implementation of the OMS program, the OGP site had fully established a process-driven culture with Process Based Leadership®. Having the process-driven foundation proved invaluable during the company's transition to OMS.

The Solution

Solutions were implemented in two distinct phases:

- **Phase 1.** Following an initial assessment of OGP operations, CSI delivered Process Based Leadership® training with a focus on creating a standardized communication process, which was then tightly integrated with a corrective actions process tool called an Action Register. CSI also created and refined scorecards that connected all leaders and teams from site leadership all the way down to the frontline leaders. Implementing the scorecard system helped establish a common business language.
- **Phase 2.** After putting into place the common communication system of the business scorecard, the OGP facility tackled the task of implementing the new OMS program, which was mandated by its corporate offices.

The Results

With Process Based Leadership® being firmly embedded in their daily operating culture, the client has seen substantial, measurable results with improving communication effectiveness and flow, increasing employee engagement and accountability, and discovering root causes when goals are not met.

The site manager reported, "When OMS launched in early 2008, every OGP entity had to make an official transition to this new system. In Q3 2008, the site became the first entity to make the full transition, and it is a direct result of having PBL as the foundation behind how we manage processes and procedures, use action registers and scorecards. The strong PBL foundation made this transition very easy. We are regarded as the company-wide leader and used as a benchmark entity for safety, operations, cost, continuous improvement and leadership."

In September 2011, the OGP site was officially selected as the Exemplar Site in Refining and Marketing in terms of its implementation and mastering of the corporation's Operating Management Systems. This equates to OGP being seen as the OMS leader in the organization and now gives them the opportunity to lead change and teach other locations how it's done.

In November 2011, OGP won two top awards at a ceremony in London. The site leader said: "We won both the Safety Excellence Helios Award and the Best of the Best Helios Award. This was the tenth year for the Group Helios Awards and we were the first team to ever win two distinct awards. I would say that a big contributor to our great workforce culture is the result of our Process Based Leadership training. I take pride in that [CSI] helped us create an environment of trust, teamwork, and accountability.

Measurable improvements include the following:

- **Better understanding of the business.** Employees now have a much clearer picture of how their team is contributing to the overall success and advancement of the business. Because of their participation in standard, nonnegotiable meetings, employees are kept informed of critical news, changes in operations, and events affecting their contributions to the bottom line. These meetings also allow them to make suggestions and ask clarifying questions of senior leaders.

- **Process integration.** By integrating Action Registers and scorecards into every meeting, each team maintains a focus on the areas in need of improvement. When necessary, a root cause analysis is conducted, and actions are assigned and later discussed in a future meeting.
- **Making corrections and getting more accomplished.** OGP has effectively reduced confusion and decreased meeting times by allowing decisions to be made more quickly and then allowing employees to make corrections outside of meetings. With 10 years of experience using Action Registers, teams have even developed a fully integrated task-tracking tool.

CASE STUDY 4
International Ink Manufacturer (IIM) Gets Great Return

The Challenge

Initially, the challenge was to improve on the monthly communication process of the Field Operations of an International Ink Manufacturer (IIM). Once Field Operations began using the Process Based Leadership methodology, it also recognized the critical issue of open-ended actions. A senior vice president explains, "As a division we were having monthly meetings via a conference call with each branch. This required my staff to physically get together for the series of conference calls, which lasted a brutal day and a half. There were travel expenses and an ongoing action item list that regularly failed to deliver us the results we needed. Some of the actions were literally open for several months."

The Solution

CSI delivered several days of Process Based Leadership® training with a focus on creating a new communication process that integrated an accountability process, with a new scorecard metrics, utilizing PBL Scorecard software to maximize efficiencies. With PBL Scorecard Remote Hosting services, Field Operations employees in more than a dozen North American locations are able to contribute to a division scorecard. Field Operations plans to expand use of the PBL Scorecard to the individual branch levels.

Prior to leveraging Process Based Leadership® and PBL Scorecard®, IIM attempted to develop a scorecard system using MS Excel. The results were less than desired as the vice president reports: "We made a weak attempt at building a scorecard using Excel spreadsheets, but the attempt ultimately failed. Our many, many action items were in multiple files. We also had issues finding all the right documents associated with our metrics and actions. Now, PBL Scorecard® has allowed us to keep all of our metrics, actions and documents all in one location, which has made managing our business more efficient."

The Results

Since officially launching the use of PBL Scorecard in January 2010, IIM has seen measurable results in reducing travel time and expenses, improving communication effectiveness, increasing accountability, and discovering root causes when goals are not met.

IIM management said it chose PBL Scorecard because "the accountability created through PBL and the software got our attention. Having everything related to the scorecard included within the software was a big plus. The cost is very reasonable as well."

Measurable improvements include the following:

- **Saving time.** Prior to Process Based Leadership implementation, IIM held monthly conference calls involving several people, taking a day and a half to complete. A vice president from IIM reports, "I estimate that we save 10–12 hours of meeting time per month versus our former process. We now meet twice monthly via webinar, each meeting lasts merely 60 to 90 minutes in total."

- **Saving money.** Related to cost savings, IIM no longer has the monthly travel expenses that often totaled as much as $5,000.
- **Getting more done.** By tying action items directly to scorecard metrics the Field Operations team is more focused on the areas in need of improvement. IIM management concludes, "We are getting better at identifying actions needed and also getting those actions done on time. With centralized data, accountability, and ability to document every step taken in a corrective action process it leads to achieving more of our metric goals. It's all in one place."

CASE STUDY 5
Private Jet Manufacturer (PJM) Reaches New Heights

Private Jet Manufacturer (PJM) is a manufacturer of private jet planes. After riding high in the late 1990s and reaching all-time highs in 2000, PJM faced a tough economy with a lot of uncertainty in a post–9/11 world. The years of 2002 and 2003 were especially challenging, resulting in a wage freeze, a plant shutdown, and the absorption of completions work from its other facility.

The Challenge

PJM's vision was to become the industry leader in customer experience, set new standards for health and safety, and reduce waste in every aspect of their operations.

The question the company faced was, "How do we get there?"

To realize its vision PJM needed first to understand its current state so it could create a strategic transformation plan and achieve its stated vision. With assistance from Competitive Solutions, Inc., a comprehensive assessment was conducted.

The assessment revealed the following in the absence of standard operating processes:

Senior management lacked an understanding of where the disconnect between leadership and employees was truly occurring.

Communication was not structured nor did it have standards. Team meetings were infrequent and random. Shift startup meetings provided little value.

Metrics, to the extent they existed, were not consistently maintained, nor did the workforce understand them. It was unclear who was responsible for gathering data, producing charts, and posting the metrics.

The Solution

Based on the stated vision and the assessment findings, PJM executed a long-term continuous improvement plan called the PJM Strategic Transformation. With a focus on Safety, Quality, Productivity, and Human Development, this plan incorporates Six Sigma, TIP Projects, a balanced scorecard, Achieving Excellence, and Process Based Leadership® (PBL) as its foundation. PJM Improvement Manager said, "[PBL is] the foundation for our PJM Strategic Transformation, establishing fundamental behaviors required of our teams in a Lean system."

The Results

With the implementation of PBL, the basis of the leadership GPS process, an organizational transformation has occurred, and people have noticed the following:

- The transformation is aligned and supportive of the business priorities.
- PJM is integrating and evolving every aspect of its business and the way it operates.
- The transformation applies simple Lean fundamentals across the entire organization for "improvement and lift."
- The transformation allows PJM to deliver predictable results to customers and stakeholders.

Customer experience survey results reveal a whole new impression of PJM. A Gallup poll shows that PJM owners are highly engaged and satisfied at all phases of their relationship with the company, including buyer satisfaction, customer delivery, and customer service. One customer's CEO commented, "The way [PJM] present[s] material to me is so professional and above board. . . . They treat me like I'm part of their family."

Measureable improvements include the following:

- **Daily communication flow.** Beginning with startup meetings, critical information cascades upward four levels within the first 90 minutes of each day. All 2,600+ employees are engaged and are able to answer these questions:
  - Did we get our work done safely?
  - Who needs help?
  - Did we get today's work done today?
- **Corrective actions are a part of daily operations.** With employees keeping a close eye on scorecards, metrics are reviewed routinely, and corrective action plans are executed to keep everyone on the right course to achieve the mission.
- **Health and safety are now "world class."** Overall safety has shown staggering improvements. Within three years, the number of annual safety incidents was reduced from 347 to only 34. PJM is now the safety leader with a very low number of cases per 200,000 hours worked. Anything below a score

of 0.5 is considered world class, and PJM now scores a 0.23. For two consecutive years, PJM was the most improved organization within their parent company.

- **The Employee Engagement Index increased to 77%.** Over the same three-year period that saw dramatic safety achievements, PJM recorded major increases in employee engagement as well. Prior to the transformation, its Employee Engagement Index was at 56%. A few years later they registered a 77% score.

CASE STUDY 6
World Class Evaporator Manufacturer Delivers Results

World Class Evaporator Manufacturer (WCEM), a privately held company, is the world's largest producer of frost-free evaporator coils and a leading global supplier of aluminum heat transfer tubing and components for appliances, HVAC, and automotive air-conditioning.

The Challenge

WCEM's senior leaders recognized a need to make performance improvements and was determined to leverage its employees' strengths through business-focused work teams and a robust communication process. Top management set its sights on "being the best" and creating a culture of empowerment and personal accountability. Additionally, it determined to set its strategic goals based on all the criteria laid out by *Industry Week* for its Top 5 Manufacturers.

The Solution

Working closely with senior leaders, CSI helped WCEM develop a comprehensive plan to implement a business alignment system called Process Based Leadership® (PBL). The plan included a transition to a team-directed workforce, the implementation of accountability processes, the creation of a Business Scorecard, and the development of a meeting-driven communication process.

Some of the tactical components of WCEM's PBL implementation include weekly communication meetings focused on performance, Business Scorecards for every team in the organization providing connectivity to the bottom line, and team problem-solving and decision-making processes to guide performance improvement efforts. All of these components are paired with auditable processes to drive business results.

The Results

WCEM aligned all its business processes in such a way that all employees have become business-performance experts. Business-focused decisions are now made at the appropriate levels by the appropriate people.

"Our employees are our greatest asset. Empowering them with bottom-line business accountability has been, and will continue to be, the key to our growth and success," proclaims WCEM president.

During a six-year period following implementation of Process Based Leadership®, WCEM's sales tripled and its profits grew by 260%. WCEM shares its financial success with all of its employees through a bonus plan based on the company's profitability and individual or departmental objectives that are tied to the company's annual return on net assets. All employees feel like they are true owners in the company.

"We should be very proud of what we've accomplished, yet never satisfied that we have reached our potential," adds the WCEM president.

WCEM was named one of *IndustryWeek*'s Top 5 Manufacturers. Previous award winners include such notables as Toyota, Merck, and Nestle.

CASE STUDY 7
Army Tactical Assault Vehicle Overhaul Repair Facility Improves Operations

Competitive Solutions, Inc., partnered with Army Tactical Assault Vehicle Overhaul Repair Facility (ATAVORF) to implement and sustain Process Based Leadership® (PBL) as a fundamental piece of its operational transformation, designed to help ATAVORF remain a leading installation for the long term.

The Challenge

In 2007, ATAVORF was seeking to improve overall daily operations efficiencies, to better serve the needs of the war fighters, and to ensure greater delivery, quality, and service to the patriots serving in Iraq and Afghanistan.

The Solution

CSI, working closely with command and staff, designed a multiyear project plan that would drive visible and auditable systems throughout every team at the depot. These systems include the following:

- A scorecard to track, maintain, and improve mission performance

- An accountability system to drive clear and concise actions both within meetings and to failing metrics on each team's scorecard
- A communication system that provides a seven-day cycle of nonnegotiable communication meetings designed to drive urgency and information throughout the entire depot
- A transformative behavioral system that defines clear expectations of engagement

These systems are the pillars of CSI's Process Based Leadership® methodology and the leadership GPS process.

CSI launched Process Based Leadership® at ATAVORF in 2008, with a mission to drive greater clarity, connectivity, and consistency throughout the installation. ATAVORF embraced the Process Based Leadership® systems as a means to secure its future and remain a top-tier member of the army's industrial base. Recognizing the criticality of efficient and dynamic support of the demanding needs of the war fighters, ATAVORF leaders embraced the PBL process to drive greater focus, urgency, and accountability ensuring greater delivery, quality, and service to the patriots serving in Iraq and Afghanistan.

The Results

As a result of great leadership and dedication to this transformation shown by all employees, the success of Process Based Leadership® has brought awards and accolades to CSI. Competitive Solutions, Inc., was honored to receive the Corporate Partnership Award at the ATAVORF Business Showcase hosted in June 2011. Being recognized in this capacity is a prestigious honor for the staff of CSI.

Shane Yount, principal with CSI, accepting this award on behalf of the CSI team, acknowledged, "ATAVORF and its dedicated team of civilians recognize that to compete in the global marketplace, one must never stop pushing forward. Challenging the way we have done business and not accepting the status quo is a core value at ATAVORF. It has been an honor for the CSI team to play a small part in assisting ATAVORF in its pursuit of performance excellence and to embrace their mission of supporting the war fighter."

The ATAVORF commanding officer said, "ATAVORF has been able to maximize our workforce's potential, reduce costs and overhead, and increase quality and customer service by initiating the skills learned through Competitive Solutions, Inc. Through the use of Process Based Leadership, ATAVORF has been able to improve our business results, communication, trust, morale and interpersonal effectiveness."

25 Leadership GPS "Tuesday Tips"

Every Tuesday, Competitive Solutions sends out a Tuesday Tip e-mail. (You can sign up for those tips at www.competitive-solutions.net.) These tips reinforce the concepts of the leadership GPS process. Here are some of the tips:

Tip 1: Empowerment or Engagement? Why Not Both?

A decade ago "empowerment" was a top buzzword, and human resources managers were searching for the best methods to provide it to their employees. What was being labeled as empowerment really only took the employees' perspective into consideration. What employees were actually asking for was the opportunity to make an impact, which from the organization's point of view means to be "engaged."

Today leading organizations are focused on increasing engagement levels and empowering their employees to make a more direct impact on the bottom line.

What's the difference?

- **Engagement**—getting it done, on time, with impact on business goals

- **Empowerment**—providing the tools, the time, and the freedom to accomplish important tasks

Tip 2: The 8 Tenets of Employee Engagement

By and large, employees in any organization want to be successful. They want to be seen as collaboratively and collectively moving their organization forward—that is, they *want* to be engaged. True employee engagement cannot occur without a defined methodology.

The key to an employee's success in becoming highly engaged is the ability to follow a model of Learn, Know, and Do. Eight tenets of employee engagement should serve as the backbone for any organization's employee engagement methodology.

The 8 tenets of employee engagement

1. Demonstrate business acumen.
2. Demonstrate and utilize continuous improvement tools.
3. Demonstrate accountability through actions.
4. Demonstrate ownership for development.
5. Demonstrate altruistic decision making.
6. Demonstrate collaborative mentoring/coaching.
7. Demonstrate a passionate self-motivation.
8. Demonstrate positive affirmation.

Tip 3: Finding Common Ground for Motivating Your Diverse Workforce

Most organizations draw strength from having a diverse workforce, often with several generations working side by side. These generations bring different views on how they work, find motivation, and achieve success.

The ability to identify and understand employees from different generations can provide leaders with a big advantage when they are looking for ways to motivate their team.

4 Workforce Generations and What Motivates Each

- **Matures (65+).** Hardworking and trustworthy, they see motivation as a moral obligation.
- **Baby boomers (46–64).** Optimistic and goal oriented, they are motivated by effecting change.
- **Gen X (31–45).** Clever and resourceful, they are motivated by having flexible responsibilities and seeking status.
- **Gen Y (Millennials, under 30).** Resilient and realistic about their futures, they are motivated by challenging and innovative work responsibilities.

Most employees want to contribute and be successful. Although individual employees draw motivation from different sources, the common ground they share is that they look to their leaders for that motivation.

Tip 4: Adjust Your Decision Making Style to Motivate Your Multi-Gen Team

Each generation views decision making in different ways. Managers today have the challenge to create a single process for making and communicating important business decisions. Without a defined and transparent process, managers run the risk of frustrating and not motivating their team members.

Decision Making by Different Generations

- **Mature (65+).** Typically expect decisions to be driven from the top down.
- **Baby boomers (46–64).** Usually expect some say in the decisions being made.
- **Gen X (31–45).** They commonly see decision making as a team-oriented activity.

- **Gen Y (under 30).** They often see decision making as highly collaborative, with only little guidance from a team leader.

Knowing how employees view the decision-making process is a great first step in the development of a trustworthy process for involving and motivating those around you.

Tip 5: Breaking Down Multi-Gen Communication Barriers

Determining practical ways to communicate with employees can be a major challenge for managers, especially with a multigenerational team. When one is leading a multigenerational team learning to understand employee backgrounds and personal communication, styles can be a great asset.

Break Down Communication Barriers

1. Learn more about each employee's personal communication preferences with an assessment tool such as D.A.R.E.
2. Identify generational differences to better understand how each employee views communication.
3. Create communication process standards to break down barriers by determining the frequency for holding meetings, the structure each meeting should have, and the roles each person should play when in a meeting.

By having a better understanding of communication styles and generational differences, managers can create standardized processes to overcome typical communication barriers.

Tip 6: Why Incentive Programs Don't Motivate Employees

With the best of intentions, many leaders throw parties, give gifts, and shell out monetary rewards in an attempt to motivate their teams. Unfortunately, such traditional incentive programs have no lasting, meaningful effect on workforce motivation levels.

By definition, one person cannot motivate another.Motivation is intrinsic. A leader can only provide an environment that is conducive and supportive of employees choosing to exhibit motivated behavior.

Employee recognition is an important ingredient for creating such an environment. The desire to be recognized by one's leaders and peers is universal. You can recognize employees in your staff meetings by doing the following:

1. Publicly thank the employee for a job well done.
2. Describe what the employee did and why that was important.
3. Explain how this action positively affects the organization's bottom line.
4. Elevate the story up the organizational chart, so that others can share in the recognition.

Tip 7: Why Your Spreadsheet Fails as a Scorecard

One of the most popular uses of spreadsheet software is for business scorecards. Is this a good decision? Electronic spreadsheets arrived in the late 1970s as a replacement for bookkeeping tasks traditionally done on paper. Are they capable of handling your scorecards in 2012?

Studies Show a Disappointing Reality

Recent studies find numerous reasons to lose faith in your spreadsheets.

- 94% of spreadsheets contain errors (Stephen G. Powell, Kenneth R. Baker, Barry Lawson, "A Critical Review of the Literature on Spreadsheet Errors")
- 57% of spreadsheet users have never received formal training ("Spreadsheet Risk Management within UK Organisations")

- 72% of spreadsheet users report having no audit process to check for accuracy ("Spreadsheet Risk Management within UK Organisations")

In light of these findings, would you feel safe in using a spreadsheet to compile your critical business data for tracking performance and making important decisions?

Tip 8: Top 3 Issues with Business Scorecards

By 2011, an estimated 85% of organizations had adopted a performance measurement system in one form or another. Although performance measurement systems are useful, one should be aware of the common issues faced with most scorecards today.

Top 3 issues with scorecards

1. **Improperly defined metrics.** With poorly defined objectives and/or targets, employees can claim confusion and avoid accountability for results.
2. **Inefficient data collection.** With weekly or monthly deadlines, most scorecards have incomplete data. Organizations struggle to keep scorecards current by assigning an administrator to drive data collection and reporting, which is costly and ineffective.
3. **Lack of standards for scorecard usage.** As soon as a scorecard is updated, it begins to age. Without an established, formal review process, organizations can't rely on the scorecard's usefulness for timely, relevant decision making.

These issues are real but can be overcome by fully implementing leadership GPS.

Tip 9: Excel-Based Scorecards Create Management Headaches

Random surveys of clients conducted by CSI have found that nearly 90% of PBL Scorecard users had previously been using Microsoft Excel for their business scorecard needs. The survey revealed some key insight into why leading organizations are making the jump from simple spreadsheet technology, such as Excel, to a modern and robust solution, such as the PBL Scorecard®.

Excel scorecard headaches include the following:

- **Maintaining accurate formulas.** Unless one is properly trained, creating complicated formulas can be very difficult. Once built, it is very easy to break formulas as well.
- **Limited access.** Only one person at a time can open the file for editing. This causes a traffic jam when dozens of people need to update their data by the same deadline.
- **Custom reporting is very time consuming.** It is tremendously difficult to create a nice presentation that includes data from multiple workbooks and sheets. It is very inefficient, especially if the report is only used once.

Tip 10: Embrace Failure as an Opportunity

Many of today's leaders cringe when it comes to identifying and discussing productivity failures with employees. Coaching opportunities are often missed because leaders have been conditioned to believe that "red is bad" when reviewing outcomes on team scorecards.

The following suggestions are important to remember when your color-coded scorecard shows a lot of red:

1. **Don't point fingers.** Poor performance on a scorecard should not be turned into a blame game session; this rarely has any positive effect on future results.

2. **Find the root cause.** In many cases, poor performance is the result of multiple factors that may not even be within your span of control. Discovering the cause will help you avoid repeating mistakes.

3. **Put on your coaching cap.** Great leaders see failing metric scores as their chance to teach, train, and develop their people. Taking this tack should improve morale and lead to increased teamwork and better performance over time.

Tip 11: Use Agendas as Your Meeting's GPS

When meetings occur without agendas, time can be wasted and employees become frustrated. Agendas are an important tool with which to move meetings and your organization in the right direction.

Agendas Serve as the Meeting's GPS

1. **Stay on the correct path.** Without an agenda to follow, it can be easy for the meeting to get off track and for valuable time to be wasted on the wrong things.

2. **Allow participants to prepare in advance.** Running a meeting without an agenda is like getting in your car without preparing for a big trip. What do you need to bring? How much time will it take?

3. **Stay within time constraints.** A good agenda should include time limits for each item on the list. Appoint a time keeper to help the participants stay focused and keep the meeting moving.

Tip 12: In a Meeting Rut? Invite an Outside Person

If it has been a while since you felt like your staff meetings were effective and meaningful, then maybe it is time to make some adjustments. Instead of muddling through wasteful brainstorming sessions on how to make improvements, why not invite an outside person?

An Outside Person Can Help You Overhaul Your Meetings

- **Get feedback.** By simply observing a meeting, making notes, and then reporting their findings, an outside person will help you identify your areas of opportunity and make recommendations.
- **Make necessary changes.** Take the outside person's suggestions and make necessary corrections.
- **Facilitate.** With the outside person's help, hold a meeting with all your adjustments and new processes. This hands-on approach will reinforce how your meetings will occur moving forward.

Tip 13: Too Many Meetings? Send a Delegate

In most organizations today, communication is cited as the biggest challenge to growing and developing businesses. In a recent assessment of a new client, we confirmed this common issue and took note when a leader said, "I've been with this company for 17 years and the director of operations for the last six. I spend at least 30 hours a week in meetings. When did 'meeting attendee' become my primary role?"

Too Many Meetings? Send a Delegate

- **More work.** Each minute you spend in a meeting is a minute taken away from your time to get your work completed. Sending a delegate gives you back more of your time.
- **Professional growth.** By sending someone on your team to participate on your behalf, you'll give that person the opportunity to learn new things and grow skills.
- **A morale booster.** Treat the delegate role with reverence and importance. If it is seen as a reward, you'll have no shortage of eager employees looking for their opportunity to be a delegate.

Tip 14: Improve Your Listening Skills in Meetings

One of the main reasons for attending meetings is to update your colleagues on performance issues and the status of various work activities. An often overlooked reason for attending meetings is to hear what those same colleagues have to say about their important initiatives and activities. It can be difficult to be a good listener if you are not properly prepared.

How to Improve Your Listening Skills in Meetings

1. **Tune out your technology.** Be ready for copious note-taking with paper and pen in hand. Turn off your laptop and smart phone to avoid distractions.
2. **Ask for clarity.** If necessary, ask for something to be repeated. Don't move to the next topic if you are unclear about what was said.
3. **Show patience and focus.** Allow others to finish their thoughts and hear what they have to say. Don't let yourself begin forming your replies until they've finished.

Tip 15: How Do You Determine Business Decisions?

Decisions, decisions, decisions. Leaders face important business decisions every day. To help you refine your decision-making skills, you can use one of several decision-making models, including six-step models, nine-step models, and even systems designed to score your decision-making accuracy. One thing is for certain, you need to have appropriate, timely, and meaningful data to help you make the best decisions.

A Business Scorecard, when done correctly, will help you strengthen your decision-making skills. Is your system optimized for decision making?

To use a scorecard in decision making, ask the following questions:

- Do I have enough data?
- Do I have too much data?

- Am I measuring the right things?
- Does my scorecard align and connect to our mission?
- Do I have a span of control over the results?
- Is my scorecard facilitating my decision making and helping me advance the business?
- Do I use a scorecard as the main driver for making decisions?

Tip 16: Solving the Dysfunction between Functional Areas

Many departments or business units perform dysfunctionally, often because they each operate with their own agendas. They form their own departmental cultures. They can even have different methods for defining and measuring success.

Quite often the most dysfunctional team in the entire organization is the senior leadership team. Since it is the group charged with the task of defining the mission and strategies, it needs to work together, operate as a unit, and provide a framework for employees to follow in pursuit of the mission.

How to Resolve Organizational Dysfunction

1. Define one organization-wide mission.
2. Develop mission-related focus areas.
3. Based on the defined focus areas, have all employees (all levels, all departments) use the same performance-tracking system for measuring results.
4. Allow tactical-level customization of specific metrics and goals, and give employees span of control to accomplish their individual pieces.

Tip 17: Four Steps to Effective Delegation

Leaders are asked to get many things accomplished with limited time and resources. They can't possibly do everything themselves; therefore, it's critical for leaders to learn how to delegate properly. Delegation is not passing the buck to others. Responsibility still lies with the leader. Effective delegation takes effort, preparation, and practice.

1.   Select the task and match it to the proper employee.
   • Consider time frame, necessary training, and ability to complete the task.
   • Use previous experiences, utilize strengths, and provide opportunity for growth.
2.   Communicate the task and gain commitment.
   • Meet to discuss the task's importance and value to the organization.
   • Explain the benefits of accomplishing the task.
   • Clearly articulate the desired outcomes, time frame, and results.
   • Confirm understanding and gain commitment.
3.   Maintain supervisory control.
   • Observe and provide feedback.
   • Review periodically and track progress.
   • Validate completion of a task.
4.   Provide recognition.
   • Recognize the contribution.
   • Set the tone for future delegation of tasks.

Tip 18: How Leaders Influence the Work Climate

A work climate is defined as the prevailing atmosphere experienced by the employees. As a leader, regardless of your formal role, you are part of what makes up the work climate. You have a direct influence over creating and maintaining the work climate you and your team members experience.

High-performing work climates are characterized as having clear communication, appropriate supervision of tasks, and a goal-focused culture in which all employees are expected to contribute.

So what does an atmosphere that is both positive and productive have?

The Three-Layered Foundation of a High-Performing Work Climate

- **Trust**. Whether given automatically or earned through exhibited behaviors, trust is an essential component of a positive work climate.
- **Honesty**. Employees look to leaders to be fair, truthful, and morally upright.
- **Respect**. To create mutual respect, leaders should exhibit dignity, courtesy, and empathy toward others. This builds a feeling of admiration and creates the high-performing work climate you need.

Tip 19: Why Employees Don't Perform

Being an effective leader is less about you and your skills and more about what you are able to get accomplished with the team around you. In short, it's all about getting things done without always doing them yourself.

Three Reasons Employees Don't Meet Performance Expectations

1. They don't know what to do.
2. They don't know how to do it.
3. They don't want to do it (lack desire or motivation).

The Solutions:

1. **What to do.** What gets measured gets done. By using a team scorecard, your employees will know what to do based on what is being measured. The metric goals on the scorecard provide focal points for the employees.

2. **How to do it.** Some leaders struggle with how to empower people to discover the "how" in solving performance issues. Using an Action Register will help leaders assign tasks and get out of the way.
3. **Want to do it.** An organization's culture plays a big part in driving high levels of motivation. At a team level, leaders can boost and sustain motivation with frequent feedback and recognition. Having weekly meetings that feature public "pats on the back" will elevate employee motivation.

Tip 20: Five Steps to Minimizing Performance Barriers

When developing and maintaining a continuous improvement culture, it is critical that leaders provide employees with a process for overcoming obstacles. Whether anticipated or unforeseen, barriers can easily derail employees' efforts and cause a decline in performance outcomes. To keep performance improvements on track, leaders can follow a practical, five-step process.

1. Agree that a barrier exists.
2. Discuss alternatives to minimizing the barrier.
3. Agree on actions to be taken to implement an alternative course of action.
4. Follow up to confirm follow-through on the actions taken.
5. Adjust operational processes to ensure the barrier remains minimized moving forward.

By helping employees face barriers head on, a leader builds trust and reinforces a continuous improvement culture. Over time, employees will become more adept at recognizing barriers, providing alternative options, and following through with corrective actions on their own.

Tip 21: How to Practice "What's Next?" Thinking

Leaders considering ways to ramp up their organization's continuous improvement outcomes can implement a myriad of different quick-fix solutions. However, one surefire way to revolutionize their organization's prevailing culture and sustain meaningful results is to adopt a forward-looking approach called "What's next?" thinking.

1. **Congratulate; then move on.** Celebrate performance improvements, but don't be content with past results. Keep an eye on future goals.
2. **Be real.** Nothing harms teamwork and trust more than unclear expectations or avoiding a discussion when failure occurs. Your team can learn from mistakes while tracking progress as best practices are discovered.
3. **Reinforce the thinking.** Whenever there's an urge to return to old methods or the team feels uneasy about changing behaviors, leaders can reinforce the new way of thinking by communicating a "from this day forward" approach in making decisions.

Sometimes simply setting the proper tone creates lasting effects to sustain successful continuous improvement initiatives. With practice, What's next? thinking will become a part of your daily dialogue and organizational culture.

Tip 22: How to Let Employees Accelerate Change

When developing and maintaining a continuous improvement (CI) culture in organizations, leaders must provide employees with a process for overcoming obstacles. Whether anticipated or unforeseen, barriers can easily derail employees' efforts and cause a decline in performance outcomes. To keep performance improvements on track, follow a practical process.

1. **Set the vision.** Within the context of a CI project, communicate a vision for what needs to be improved.

2.   **Delegate assignments.** Without mandating decisions on how to proceed, assign portions of the project to individuals on the team. Set some milestone targets to ensure action.

3.   **Allow employees to problem solve.** When employees are empowered to decide how to accomplish their piece of the project, they will feel a true ownership stake in the outcomes. Naturally, this leads to more engagement and energy put into follow-through. This is the secret formula for accelerating change, because Ownership = Energy.

4.   **Review and recognize.** Publicly review the outcomes of the finished project and provide ample applause for a job well done. This creates a positive, can-do atmosphere for the next project.

When managing a continuous improvement project, accelerate the project's completion by stating the vision, setting milestone goals, then stepping aside and letting the employees accomplish the rest.

Tip 23: Boost Accountability Levels

Employees at all levels want to contribute and be successful. They like to be involved in team efforts and to be seen as someone pulling their fair share of the weight. Leaders can set the stage for employees and provide a boost to accountability levels by applying a practical, four-step process.

Your 4-step Accountability Booster Process

1.   **Identify accountability.** Know it when you see it. Create a way to bring attention and visibility to employees' behaviors as they take on various tasks. For each task, identify what is to be done and by whom, and set a due date for completion.

2.   **Monitor accountability.** Next, track accountability levels based on actual versus intended follow-through

on assignments. Over time, you'll build up a history of tangible data that will provide you with a way to see behavior patterns. Recognizing these behavior patterns allows you to address any accountability issues.

3. **Encourage accountability.** Sustain high accountability levels by frequently and publicly patting people on the back for their hard work and follow-through. This positive reinforcement is great for morale and motivation.

4. **Normalize accountability.** Under your leadership, high levels of accountability will become the cultural norm by your having applied enough focus, encouragement, and lead-by-example modeling of the expected behaviors.

After setting the stage and providing guidance, your team culture will evolve and enable sustained high levels of accountability. Over time, being accountable will come naturally and require less and less hands-on effort from leadership.

Tip 24: Prioritizing Assignments

Many leaders don't have difficulty assigning tasks to people on their team. The real issues begin when they fail to provide additional support and guidance on the follow-through and completion of those assignments.

How to Help Employees Prioritize Assignments

1. **Set due dates.** Timing is a major component to consider when deciding which task should be completed first. Setting appropriate due dates will naturally provide an employee with a sense of urgency to complete their tasks. Without a set date for each task, you are unable to provide guidance on which to do next.

2. **Know the bottom-line impact.** Placing a score value on individual tasks allows employees to see the direct impact

they have on the success or failure of the business. The more valuable an assignment, the more likely it is to draw attention and priority over other, less important assignments.

3.   **Calculate the resources required.** Along with due dates and values scores, factor in how much effort is required to complete each individual task. Some assignments require far more people, time, money, and education than others.

By setting appropriate due dates, understanding the value to the business, and factoring the overall effort required for each assignment, employees will have an easier time prioritizing their assignments.

Tip 25: Warning Signs of Unmotivated Employees

Many employees are intrinsically motivated. They want to see their organization succeed, and they want to be a factor in that success. However, several recent studies on employee engagement shine a light on the adverse effects of poorly defined processes, burdensome red tape, and conflicting messages from senior leaders. These obstacles lead to a workforce that is frustrated and eventually unmotivated.

Three Behavioral Phases of Unmotivated Employees

*   **Burning out.** After several months of overcoming obstacle after obstacle, highly engaged employees begin to grow weary of exerting so much effort to get all their work done. They begin recognizing the disparity between their efforts and the efforts of their least engaged coworkers.
*   **Giving up.** After becoming frustrated with the difficulties and high levels of efforts needed to succeed, many employees practice selective engagement. This means that they start choosing which assignments they will complete while abandoning others completely.

224

- **Jumping ship.** When their engagement levels bottoms out, employees begin seeking other places to apply their talents and rejuvenate their careers. This can cause an organization to lose its most promising talent.

According to a recent study by the Hay Group, as many as 76% of your employees are making plans to move on to their next employer if they are unmotivated and not enabled to succeed. This information alone should alarm anyone in a leadership position! The solution is to engage employees in a meaningful manner, such as through the leadership GPS process.

Bibliography

"Basic Diversity Presentation," Al Vivian. B.A.S.I.C. Diversity, Inc.

"Closing the Engagement Gap: A Road Map for Driving Superior Business Performance," 2008 Towers Perrin Global Workplace Study.

Cultural Intelligence: A Guide to Working with People from Other Cultures, Brooks Peterson. Nicholas Brealey Publishing 2004.

"Do Cultures Segment Time Differently," Lawrence T. White, Ph.D., *Psychology Today*, Jan. 27, 2012. http://www.psychologytoday.com/blog/culture-conscious/201201/do-cultures-segment-time-differently.

Kiss, Bow, or Shake Hands, Terri Morrison and Wayne A. Conaway. Adams Media 2006.

People Styles at Work: Making Bad Relationships Good and Good Relationships Better, Robert Bolton and Dorothy Grover Bolton. AMACOM 1996.

Productivity: The Human Side, Robert R. Blake and Jane Srygley Mouton. AMACOM 1981.

Index

Education, scorecards for, 8–9, 30
Ego, leadership and, 78–79, 81, 83
Electronic scorecards, 110–111
E-mail, 126–127
Employees. *See also* Engagement;
    People
  accelerating change, 221–222
  accomplishments, 158
  business knowledge of, 157
  engagement of, 208
  incentive programs and, 210–211
  jobs and, 22
  leadership and character of,
    84–85
  leadership tips for, 208, 210–211,
    219–222, 224–225
  performance of, 219–220
  psychology, 220–221
  success of, 208
  unmotivated, 224–225
Employment, conditions, 68–69
Empowerment
  definition of, 208
  engagement and, 16–17
  leadership tips for, 207–208
Engagement
  accountability and, 17, 148–149
  action register and, 139
  assessment of, 18–20
  broken, 15–16
  causes of, 17–18
  characteristics of, 18
  corrective action plans and
    collective, 141
  defining, 16–18, 207
  empowerment and, 16–17
  example of, 13–15

  improving performance and,
    143–152, 220
  leadership style and, 77
  leadership tips for, 207–208
  listening process, 61–64, 216
  performance and, 14–15, 143–152,
    220
  personal action register, 117–123,
    130
  selective, 149
  statistics on, 113
  tenets of employee, 208
  work environment and, 17
  of workforce, 13–20
Entitlement, 155–157
Ethics, leadership and, 87
Executives, retirement of, 4–5
Expectations
  behavioral, 18, 44, 65
    action register and, 139
    cultural diversity and, 44
    defining, 66–67
    negotiable, 69–71, 113–114, 120
    nonnegotiable, 68–69, 113–114,
      120, 133
  behavioral, SBI, 74–75, 88, 160–161
Expressive (D.A.R.E.), 59–61
Eye contact, 43, 169

Facilitation, scorecards for, 9, 10
Failure
  leadership and, 85
  leadership tips for, 213–214
Feedback, 70
  giving, 75–76
  listening process and, 62
  receiving, 76

About the Authors

The authors are principals of the international consulting firm Competitive Solutions, Inc., which has offices in Raleigh, North Carolina, and Atlanta, Georgia, and serves clients in North America, Europe, and the Pacific Rim. *Leading Your Business Forward: Aligning Goals, People, and Systems for Sustainable Success* is their fifth book.

Leading Your Business Forward describes a proven management system that a number of the world's top-performing companies and organizations have adopted for sustained success. These include GlaxoSmithKline, the United States Army, Harley Davidson Motor Company, Boar's Head Provisions Co., Inc., Agrium, and Lockheed Martin, to name a few.

For more information, visit the firm's website at www.competitive-solutions.net.